Does God Exist?

Examining Evidence in Support Of
a Christian Worldview

G. Todd Brimm, M.A., M.DIV.

WESTBOW
PRESS®
A DIVISION OF THOMAS NELSON
& ZONDERVAN

WestBow Press books may be ordered through booksellers or by contacting:

WestBow Press
A Division of Thomas Nelson & Zondervan
1663 Liberty Drive
Bloomington, IN 47403
www.westbowpress.com
844-714-3454

ISBN: 978-1-6642-6130-3 (sc)
ISBN: 978-1-6642-6129-7 (hc)
ISBN: 978-1-6642-6131-0 (e)

Library of Congress Control Number: 2022905097

Print information available on the last page.

WestBow Press rev. date: 04/06/2022

When they had finished eating, Jesus said to Simon Peter, "Simon son of John, do you love me more than these?"

"Yes, Lord," he said, "you know that I love you."

Jesus said, "Feed my lambs."

Again, Jesus said, "Simon son of John, do you love me?"

He answered, "Yes, Lord, you know that I love you."

Jesus said, "Take care of my sheep."

The third time he said to him, "Simon son of John, do you love me?"

Peter was hurt because Jesus asked him the third time, "Do you love

me?" He said, "Lord, you know all things; you know that I love you."

Jesus said, "Feed my sheep.

John 21:15-17 NIV

Contents

Preface

A recent *Barna* poll revealed an alarming statistic in that a significant number of young women and men are not only leaving home after high school graduation but are also leaving their faith and defining themselves as an atheist. There certainly could be any number of reasons why the number of people in Generation Z who proclaim that there is no God has doubled from Millennials. Is the Gen-Z generation twice as smart as Millennials? I'm not sure if data would support such an argument, but younger people are seemingly having a crisis of faith and the answers to these collective crises most likely are associated with their view of the world.

There are a lot of external pressures on this generation from social media to socio-political issues. These external pressures weigh upon the hearts and minds of many in today's culture, but especially those who have a faith-based background. How does a book compiled almost two millennia ago bring relevance and inform social, political, and other issues at the forefront of today's generation? Moreover, another cultural variable facing so many today is *Truth*. While certainly many generations have had some collective encounter with the concept of truth, it appears today, that truth has to be established not in the substance of an argument, but the potential of the argument to offend others.

Fortunately, *Truth* always has and always will exist. Truth at times has been hidden by a deeply held belief and when it is ignored there are consequences both individually as well as collectively within society. To have or even question a truth claim it helps tremendously if you have a worldview that presupposes that there is a creator, namely God, behind our universe and specifically, the world that we live in. Such a basic approach to having a worldview builds upon necessary interrelated fundamental tenets that impact every aspect of our lives and most likely, many key topics in any class that you might take at a university or college.

The goal of this book is not to "prove" God exists, but rather to provide evidence to the reader that if taken objectively and contrasted with the fundamental arguments of atheists, it is more likely than not that a creator is behind our amazing universe and all life on our planet. Of course, the ultimate question is, why is the idea of God or a creator so threatening to so many people, especially people within academic and scientific communities. One could fall in disdain in some circles more quickly by acknowledging they believed in the God of the Bible than if they had admitted to being a drug addict, alcoholic, or even criminal. Why is there an innate vehemence toward the idea of God?

It has been the experience of some people of faith that they have been bullied or held in intellectual contempt while attending schools, universities, and other institutions which were initially established as platforms for the free expression of ideas. The frequent result of this contempt has been young people walking away from their faith when faced with a seemingly insurmountable argument. Arguments by people who should be encouraging intellectual inquiry have formed a *bulwark of science* that is nothing more than a one-dimensional façade, a picture of a wall held up by people with a materialist or naturalist worldview chanting in a cult-like manner, *"science says!"* Instead of investigating the wall or testing its strength, young women and men look at its height from a distance and simply walk away in despair and abandon their beliefs or convictions in God.

This book is a collection of significant amounts of research to identify, classify, and present evidence for the reader. Scientific and historical evidence, as well as the intellectual prowess of intelligent philosophers from different worldviews, including atheism. The work in these pages is almost exclusively from the intellectual efforts of scholarly people in their respective fields. I have arranged, formatted, and provided a context in a brief and succinct manner so this book can and will be read. It certainly is not all of the evidence nor is the evidence fully exhausted or agued. Like any crime scene, the evidence presented consists of initial pieces of information that speak to the investigator and enable him or her to build a case for a trial.

When a person is charged with a serious crime, there are typically two stages in the criminal justice process. Initially, there is a probable cause hearing to determine if there is enough evidence to move forward to an actual felony trial. A probable cause hearing is measured on the standard of a *"preponderance of the evidence,"* or more likely than not that a felony crime occurred. However, in an actual criminal trial, the state must establish evidence at a higher standard or, *"beyond a reasonable doubt,"* to attain a conviction. Perhaps the evidence in this book will enable you to achieve a level of evidence beyond a reasonable doubt, but the goal here is to initially gain or regain confidence that the evidence supports theism as being a more logical answer than atheism as an explanation for our world and the life that is in it.

However, this book would be incomplete if the intellectual loop was not closed on the final analysis. If you believe that the evidence for a Creator or God is sufficiently established, then you should ask follow-up questions. "Has that Creator communicated with his creation and can we understand or know what that communication is?" The culmination of this book, once the evidence has been presented, is to challenge the reader to, of all things, consider Christ. The man who, based on the evidence, walked on this earth, died, and then rose again and who is the absolute revelation of God. Jesus said, if you have seen me, you have seen the Father. As far as the continuum of evidence analysis, my former pastor once said, if you can grasp Genesis 1:1, "In the beginning, God created the heavens and the earth," then the rest of the Bible is pretty easy to believe. So, here we are, our universe, our planet, our lives… they either all spontaneously occurred out of nothing, or there is indeed what the writer of John called, "the Logos," the Word.

Introduction

Does God exist? It is a valid question that people have been asking throughout history. There is nothing wrong with questions and there is nothing wrong in dealing with our doubts. Unfortunately, the question of God's existence is no longer as much an intellectual question, but a cultural mandate that assumes he does not, or at least, that he has no relevance in our lives other than in a periphery manner. Almost two decades ago an aggressive, anti-theist movement called "the new-atheist" put a few outspoken men on a global platform to vociferously argue that there is not a god and that anyone who believes in God is committing intellectual terrorism.

The influence that the "new-atheist" movement had on western culture or within academia is simply unknown. Millions of books have been sold supporting atheism, debates on colleges and universities have been waged, and of course, online sources like *YouTube* have developed into a digital battleground for arguments on the validity of theism. All of this information was critical to analyzing evidentiary arguments for this book. All of that information presented in the previous media platforms is why this book was written. When I engaged in this intellectual challenge, I had anticipated being provided with some arguments that I would have to grapple with intellectually on a deep level, even with a four-year graduate degree in theology. However, such was not the case.

As a career law enforcement officer and military historian, I am very familiar with identifying patterns of evidence, methods of operation, and operational strategy. It soon became apparent that the primary attack that the "new-atheists" were waging against the existence of God was primarily an emotional one, not an intellectual argument or the result of genuine inquiry. Of course, the new-atheists admit that the trigger to launching their opposition to God or religion was the terrorist attacks against America on September 11, 2001. The motivation for their self-proclaimed calling was anger and hatred for what happened in the name of religion. However, emotions, for anyone who has a basic understanding of how our brain works, are not complimentary to intellectual thought, but rather switch off the prefrontal cortex where mental processes operate. In other words, the more emotional that we become, the less intellect we use when analysis is necessary.

The new-atheist movement did have some intellectual backing from some prominent atheists in the scientific community, although far less outspoken. A movement to oust God out of natural philosophy (science) had started in the eighteenth century and this movement has had a cascading effect throughout the twentieth century that will become evident as you read through the chapters of this book. However, even leading physicists, cosmologists, and other scientists who argued against the existence of God did so in a very perfunctory way. As I engaged the arguments of a "new-atheist" movement I assumed that individuals from scientific and philosophical backgrounds would have a bolstered argument against the existence of God. That assumption was never realized. In the early 1980s *Wendy's* had an iconic commercial of a little old lady walking up to a restaurant counter only to lift the bun on her hamburger and shout out, *"Where's the beef!"* Those words came to my mind as I began attempting to consider the arguments presented by these erudite men that were purported to have "proved God did not exist."

What you will be reading in this book is largely the summary of the evidence presented by these outspoken atheists as well as the academic work of some great men of science who do believe in God. The facts, quotes, or contexts of statements and conclusions by atheists have not been changed or altered because the stronger I can present or clarify their argument, the stronger the case is made for the evidence of God, not the contrary. Moreover, the evidence presented by scientists and philosophers who either hold to a view that there is a Creator or that there is intelligence behind our universe was also evaluated and verified with other research, which involved much inquiry and learning.

Hopefully, this book will start you on a self-learning journey yourself, but its primary intent is to encourage you and to erase any fears that may have been impressed upon you by others who, with some modicum of evidence, claim that there is no God. Just because teachers or professors have two or three initials after their name does not mean that they speak with all authority on any given topic, let alone every topic that arises in a classroom. When the evidence presented to you is approached in an objective, fact-finding way, you will discover that God is not hiding in the dark recesses of space, but his fingerprint is clearly on his creation – especially you. Science, logic, and reason argue for that truth claim, not against it. Finally, if you are a self-proclaimed atheist or agnostic, the same effort will reveal the same results if the evidence is not suppressed based on a personal opinion or the desired outcome. You owe it to yourself to respond to the most important question in life in a manner that is truly worthy of the question – eternity depends on it.

Glossary

Agnosticism: the belief that humans cannot know of the existence of anything beyond the phenomena of their own experience.

Atheism: The denial of metaphysical beliefs in God or spiritual beings.

Beyond a Reasonable Doubt: an evidentiary standard that is greater than 51%, requires beyond a reasonable doubt, closer to 100%.

Blind-Faith: Belief without true understanding, perception, or discrimination.

Creationist: Someone who believes in a God who is the creator of the universe.

Darwinism: A theory of biological evolution from one single organism.

Eugenics: the study of how to arrange reproduction within a human population to increase the occurrence of heritable characteristics regarded as desirable.

Evidence-Based: Decisions or trust based on evidence.

Faith: From Latin *Fides*; Faith, trust, loyalty, or fidelity.

Intelligent Design: A theory that holds that certain features of the universe and living things are best explained by an intelligent cause. (Not to be confused with creationism).

Macroevolution: major evolutionary change. The term applies mainly to the evolution of whole taxonomic groups over long periods.

Materialism: The doctrine that nothing exists except matter and its movement and modifications.

Microevolution: evolutionary change within a species or small group of organisms, especially over a short period.

Naturalism: The idea or belief that only natural laws and forces operate in the universe (as opposed to supernatural ones).

Neo-Darwinism: A modern version of Darwin's theory of evolution by natural selection, incorporating the findings of genetics.

New-Atheism: A contemporary intellectual movement uniting outspoken atheists; anti-theism.

Preponderance of the Evidence: a type of evidentiary standard used in a burden of proof analysis. Under the preponderance standard, the burden of proof is met when the party with the burden convinces the fact finder that there is a greater than 50% chance that the claim is true.

Skepticism: Doubt as to the truth of something.

Acknowledgements

I started my personal research into the "theism vs atheism" debate more than two years ago having never taken an apologetics class in four years of full-time graduate studies in theology. However, the informal learning from the resources made available such as *YouTube*, non-profit ministries, and publications was to me just as challenging and rewarding as my formal classroom experiences at both the graduate and doctoral level. I am grateful to several wonderful people for their dedication to science and faith. I will share my gratitude in no special order:

Dr. John Lennox, mathematician, and scientist from Cambridge and Oxford who is the author of multiple books and whose kind, brilliant engagements with leading atheists continually serve as a light on a hill.

Dr. Steven Meyer with the *Discovery Institute*, also from Cambridge, has spearheaded an intelligent design movement and contributed greatly to academia as an exceptional scientist. His ministry of outreach and teaching was instrumental to my intellectual development.

Dr. Frank Turek with *Cross-Examined*. Dr. Turek has a phenomenal outreach to so many young women and men in academia is amazing and your ministry was an inspiration to write this book.

Dr. James Tour, leading organic chemist with more than 700 peer-reviewed research publications and multiple patents in your field. Your knowledge is only surpassed by your love for Christ.

...the people living in darkness
have seen a great light;
on those living in the land of the shadow of death
a light has dawned.'
"From that time on Jesus began to preach,
'Repent, for the kingdom of heaven has come near.'"
Matthew 4:12–17

1 Deliberate Skepticism

It is common in atheistic circles for naturalists or materialists to boldly proclaim themselves as "skeptics" when it comes to God or the supernatural. Too often, skeptics are skeptical only about things related to God and they leave no room for being a skeptic concerning their worldview. It has become routine for skeptics to be entertained about the argument for a Creator, or God, in that they simply listen and find some infinitesimal weak point in a person's argument or ask some complex question that a layperson cannot sufficiently answer and then assume to tear down an entire structure by removing one brick.

Skeptics have typically not been forced to answer the important questions about reality or truth claims within their worldview. Their worldview permits for a universe consisting of time, matter, and energy to spontaneously appear all at once in perfect proportion and at a perfect rate of acceleration. If that is not enough, within that miraculous universe, skeptics who proclaim themselves as atheists are not at all skeptical that life was yet another spontaneous creation with just the right chemicals and with whatever spark created animation from non-living matter. There are tremendous gaps and imaginative theories that derive from atheism such as the multiverse or the anthropic principle that cannot begin to be quantified or observed, let alone tested in a scientific method.

There is nothing wrong with experiencing or dealing with doubt. People in all faith systems, including atheism, experience doubt and uncertainty. However, there are multiple approaches to skepticism with the most utilitarian being the application of skepticism as an approach to doubting and questioning that leads to greater understanding.[1] Labeling oneself as a skeptic and closing the door on an argument without conducting a further inquiry into potentially valid claims about truth or reality is intellectual suicide, not skepticism. Skepticism, as it is so often applied today, is nothing more than operationalizing confirmation bias and there is no virtue in such an approach. Individuals who gloat about being a skeptic on the most important questions in life – God, the afterlife, morality, purpose, etc. – and make no effort to frame or answer these questions within a cogent, applicable worldview – are the embodiment of the characteristics that they accuse people of faith of having.

The reality is that no one will ever "prove" that God exists, at least not in our present age. Instead, a valid inquiry seeks to identify and classify evidence for the existence of God or intelligent design in our universe. Skeptics who ask for "proof that God exists" often ask for the impossible because they do not want to arrive at that conclusion. However, examining evidence that there is an intelligence to our universe and life on earth follows similar logic of observing evidence in processes that we observe in operation today. This was precisely the forensic approach that Charles Darwin engaged in for his scientific studies. Darwin was examining evidence of species evolving within species and he incorrectly interpreted that evidence as supporting his predisposed theory that all life emerged from a single-cell organism. Individuals who subscribe to a belief in intelligent design, for example, examine processes as they occur today and the requirement of a mind to produce complex, information-based DNA that far exceeds any complex code. This is the approach to forensic analysis.

A jury who is presented with physical evidence does not prove that a crime occurred. Jurors merely conclude whether or not there is sufficient evidence to remove reasonable doubt about the crime and then render a verdict on the accused based on that evidence.

Unfortunately, American justice has had a historical record of viewing guilt or innocence, based not entirely on evidence, but also on other factors problematic in a society that hinders equality. Similarly, a blind skeptic will not entertain scientific evidence concerning the argument for intelligent design, and not for a Creator, and therefore he or she is never able to come to an accurate verdict on evidence that is presented. There is nothing virtuous about closing your mind to a possibility of a Creator or intelligence behind our universe and the life that it hosts. Virtue, it has been argued, only comes when a given trait is properly applied, the knowledge that you obtain from formal and informal learning must be applied critically to all arguments.

It is virtuous for a firefighter to run into a burning structure and rescue someone. It is not virtuous to run into a burning structure to get some material object such as a game system or car keys. It is virtuous for an Air Force Pararescue Operator to conduct a high-altitude parachute jump to rescue a downed pilot. It is not virtuous for a thrill-seeker to throw a parachute out of a plane and then jump out after it to reenact a movie scene. Likewise, skepticism is only virtuous when it has a valid approach to doubt involving logic and objectivity in support for or against an argument. Skepticism involves considering the weight of evidence from a distance and then closing that distance with intellectual prowess to see what verdict for the evidence logic demands.

Positively Skeptical

The philosophical school of thought called "logical positivism" has served as a barrier wall for twentieth-century atheists as it has shielded both naturalists and strict materialists from seeking answers to hard-pressed questions about God or the supernatural. Logical positivism, sometimes referred to as logical empiricism, is the belief that reduces human knowledge down to empirical facts that can only be tested by science. The most important aspect of logical positivism, at least from the vantage point of a skeptic, is the application regarding truth claims.[2] A truth claim that cannot be tested or evaluated empirically remains untenable to a self-identified skeptic... or does it?

A frequent saying, "You cannot put God in a test tube to prove he exists," stands as a reason or excuse why many atheists refuse to entertain the God hypothesis that was eliminated from a naturalistic calculus in the nineteenth century. While the *Scientific Revolution* in the sixteenth century included symmetry between faith in a Creator and natural philosophy, or what we now call science, three centuries later, scientists, began to expel God from scientific knowledge if anything, as a Prime Reality. They began to assume that the universe had always existed and would consider Genesis 1:1, *In the beginning, God created the heavens and the earth,* as superstition or religious rhetoric. An eternal universe eliminates the need for an explanation of "how" in a given cosmological theory. Skepticism about God is easier to maintain whenever you live in a universe that has "always been," but now that Carl Sagan, and so many other cosmologists, have been proven wrong, the skeptic is required to either ignore new evidence or develop alternative theories that are currently afoot about how something came from nothing.

Einstein could not fathom a universe that was not eternal and therefore he had to consider a force that countered the drawing force of gravity. To address this requirement in his fieldwork he inserted a variable (*lambda*) to represent a cosmological constant that was equal to the force of gravity. Einstein had to add this variable to complete his field equation in the *General Theory of Relativity,* sometimes referred to as *The Standard Model.* It would be another fifteen years before Einstein experienced a paradigm shift in his thinking about a steady-state universe.

Einstein made a trip to the Griffith Observatory in 1931 to meet with Edwin Hubble. During this trip, his examination of the redshift of distant galaxies moving away from each other resulted in incontrovertible evidence that the universe was not eternal because the galaxy was moving outward. Because the universe is moving outward, when you logically rewind this outward expansion the universe eventually collapses into what is known as a singularity. Einstein would later confide with close friend and colleague Sir Arthur Eddington who tried to equivocate his response by saying, "I have no philosophical axe to grind, but the notion to a Beginning is repugnant to me. The expanding universe is preposterous, incredible. It leaves me cold."[3]

These brilliant scientists did not abandon the existence of a Creator and a beginning of the universe because they could not test a theory, they never got so far as to consider the question or develop a theory around a beginning that necessitated a Creator. They did not consider the evidence towards a theory for a Creator because it did not fit into their view of how the universe operated. Eddington's response to Einstein's findings was not a philosophical axe, it was an emotional one because it was seemingly tied to a deep-seated need to believe in a universe that was perpetual and thus eliminated the need for a beginning and the need for a Creator.

What is important here is not the scientific question of whether or not God exists, but whether or not there was a beginning to our universe. Because cosmologists presupposed that there was no God who could have created the universe the necessary conclusion was that the universe always existed and so too did time and matter. As it will be referenced in future chapters, this bold assertion by atheistic scientists costs valuable years of research because of false assumptions that the universe did not have a beginning.

Atheist Richard Dawkins, a leading intellectual among modern-day atheists, and someone whose name you will see often in this book because of his status as a leading, outspoken atheist, has taken a very similar approach to biological systems on earth. He excludes any plausible explanation that a Creator or intelligent mind could be behind the complexities of life on earth. He qualifies his belief in strictly naturalistic terms in that complex life on earth only "gives the appearance of design."[4] Although he once expressed in an interview that it was possible that intelligence outside of planet earth could have played a role in seeding life on planet earth, he ascribed that intelligence to aliens.[5]

Further research will reveal that Richard Dawkins has nowhere near the intellectual humility of his iconic naturalist, Charles Darwin. Darwin identified weaknesses and issues within his theory, as well as a standard to invalidate his theory based on evidence, all the while ardent Darwinian evolutionists hold that there are no weaknesses in evolutionary theory. In all actuality, developments in science continue to highlight significant problems with Darwinian evolution. The advancements of both science and technology have presented highly complex discoveries within the human body.

A deeper analysis of atheists like Richard Dawkins finds that their atheism was formed well before they earned a graduate degree in their field of study. Because their atheism was *a priori* to their academic work, it cannot be concluded that scientific inquiry in their field resulted in them becoming an atheist. Atheists who subscribe to a naturalist or materialist worldview too often let their worldview interpret their approach to conducting a scientific inquiry, not vice-versa. Harvard geneticist Richard Lewinton framed it well when he wrote,

> *"Our willingness to accept scientific claims that are against common sense is the key to an understanding of the real struggle between science and the supernatural. We take the side of science despite the patent absurdity of some of its constructs, in spite of its failure to fulfill many of its extravagant promises of health and life, in spite of the tolerance of the scientific community for*

unsubstantiated just-so stories, because we have a prior commitment, a commitment to materialism. It is not that the methods and institutions of science somehow compel us to accept a material explanation of the phenomenal world, but, on the contrary, that we are forced by our a priori adherence to material causes to create an apparatus of investigation and a set of concepts that produce material explanations, no matter how counter-intuitive, no matter how mystifying to the uninitiated. Moreover, that materialism is absolute, for we cannot allow a Divine Foot in the door."[6]

Best-selling author Dr. David Berlinski came to very similar conclusions on atheistic inquiry and its scientific pretensions when responding to Richard Dawkins' book, *The God Delusion*, by asking these rhetorical questions about the boldness of the scientific community as it relates to naturalist ideologies in his counter-argument from his book, *The Devil's Delusion*,

"Has anyone provided proof of God's inexistence? Not even close. *Has quantum cosmology explained the emergence of the universe or why it is here?* Not even close. *Have our sciences explained why our universe seems to be fine-tuned to allow for the existence of life?* Not even close. *Are physicists and biologists willing to believe in anything so long as it is not religious thought?* Close enough. *Has rationalism and moral thought provided us with an understanding of what is good, what is right, and what is moral?* Not close enough. *Has secularism in the terrible 20*[th] *century been a force for good?* Not even close, to being close. *Is there a narrow and oppressive orthodoxy in the sciences?*

Close enough. *Does anything in the sciences or their philosophy justify the claim that religious belief is irrational?* Not even in the ballpark. *Is scientific atheism a frivolous exercise in intellectual contempt?* Dead on."[7]

A review of the relevant scientific literature reveals that there is intellectual contempt among atheists in things about intelligent design or God. Atheists operate in their specific field with a commitment to the naturalist or materialist worldview with assurance and resolve. The bold proclamation of being an atheist is often held up as a banner intended to demonstrate skepticism and intellectual superiority within academia and the overall scientific community. Students are pressured to go along to get along if they hope to be successful in academia as students. This pressure results in a stunted intellectual discussion in academia as well as potential professional development as a scientist.

The Acid Test

In his book *Stealing From God: Why Atheists Need God to Make Their Case*, Dr. Frank Turek of *Cross Examined* argues that the foundation an atheist uses to argue against God is in fact God himself. It is a logical conclusion that former atheist C.S. Lewis was able to arrive. Nevertheless, atheists such as Sam Harris and the late Christopher Hitchens declared their vehement hatred of anything religious because of their view of religion and God. Christopher Hitches would argue vociferously that there cannot be a god because there is too much evil in the world. However, as you will read in later chapters, you need a moral agent and a higher standard by which to compare "good" with "evil" in such an argument. Without God, there can be no "good" by which to compare our perception of evil with philosophically speaking.

Another area where atheism destroys its own argument is that the logical conclusion of atheism leads us to doubt the rational process needed to do science. Dr. John Lennox of Oxford University argues that it is not science and God that conflict, but rather science and atheism because atheists have chosen a worldview that undermines the rationality needed to do science.[8] Lennox's argument falls in line with noted philosopher John Gray who wrote, "Modern humanism is the faith that through science humankind can know the truth and so be free. But if Darwin's theory of natural selection is true, this is impossible. The human mind serves evolutionary success, not truth."[9] Likewise, Alvin Plantinga argued, "if [Richard] Dawkins is right, that we're the product of mindless, unguided natural processes, then he has given us strong reason to doubt the reliability of human cognitive faculties and therefore inevitably to doubt the validity of any belief that they produce – including Dawkins' own atheism."[10] Even atheist Thomas Nagel arrived at a very similar conclusion when he wrote, "...evolutionary naturalism implies that we shouldn't take any of our convictions seriously including the scientific world picture on which evolutionary naturalism itself depends."[11]

Dawkins has proclaimed from a scientific platform "that there is no meaning, purpose or even free will in the world which results, in his own words as "blind pitiless indifference," but this statement is precisely why atheism has been referred to as an intellectual acid that burns through everything when applied to any argument for atheism. In the view of the atheist, atheism destroys the argument for theism, but when it is brought to its logical conclusions, no worldview survives. The atheist who makes an intellectual stand against God based on naturalism or materialism does so with his or her feet firmly planted in mid-air and no foundation to stand on. Atheism is a logical fallacy that starts with nothing and ends with nothing, all to say that there is nothing meaningful – no purpose, no mind, no absolute moral standard, and of course, no God.

Critical Thinking

Critical thinking is the "art of thinking about thinking."[12] It is engaging the thought process proactively, not merely responding with emotional stimuli that often accompany a strongly held worldview, especially when that worldview is threatened. If you are a student, whether high school, college, or graduate school, critical thinking is an essential tool that should be applied in all of your classes. *The Stanford Encyclopedia of Philosophy* quotes John Dewey, the "Father of American Education," who defined critical thinking as, "active, persistent and careful consideration of any belief or supposed form of knowledge in the light of the grounds that support it, and the further conclusions to which it tends."[13] The active and persistent traits of critical thinking imply that it is a continual process that is compared with not only existing evidence but new information in a continuous cycle. How dull does critical thinking become when we embrace our bias and a fractured or inconsistent worldview that does not permit the inquiry of the most challenging questions in life, questions that science in and of itself cannot answer.

Critical thinking, according to Dewey, also has a broad utility that should be applied to any belief system. To put it succinctly, critical thinking involves a consistent application of any existing evidence, for or against, a particular view, regardless of what that view involves. Any learning environment where students are not free to engage issues or problems based on a collection of quality evidence and come to logical conclusions without fear of retribution is lacking in a critical thinking process. Any learning environment where students are not encouraged to challenge their views or provide counterpoints to views presented by others is stagnant to intellectual growth. Critical thinking means that the "thinker" is collecting arguments for and against claims of validity or truth, much the same way a juror listens to a prosecution and defense team engage in intellectual battles in a courtroom.

Critical thinking is the process of constant input, evaluation, and assessment of information in a logically consistent cyclical manner. This is precisely where atheism, with naturalism or materialism serving as its foundation, completely fails intellectual scrutiny. The complete lack of objectivity as it relates specifically to intelligent design and theism is not the result of critical thinking, but the embracing of a personal bias that is closely guarded within academic circles and defended with great resolve. Academic institutions, which should serve as institutions of critical thought, have too often become intellectually bankrupt because they lack academic freedom and frequently only develop biases more along the lines of group-think.

Bias

Everyone has a bias. A bias is a logical starting point when encountering issues and realizing that we have a tendency for or against an idea in a way that influences objectivity. There are two contexts when considering bias. There are concerns of bias within organizations that speak primarily about diversity and working with people from different backgrounds. There are also issues of bias relating to scientific inquiry, which is the focus here. Bias in research can be intentional or unintentional and it occurs whenever there is a deviation in the collection, analysis, or interpretation of data.[14] While bias in research would normally be considered unethical and misleading, the realization is that a naturalist approaches scientific inquiry with a bias that the universe is a closed system. The result of this bias is a substantial loss of objectivity involving scientific inquiry related to the exquisite fine-tuning of our universe or the complex information that resulted in DNA and RNA code required for life.

In contrast, individuals who subscribe to the view that some form of mind or intelligence is behind the complexities that science has no answer for is also a bias, as it assumes that nature alone cannot sufficiently answer the key questions of origin. Intelligent design is an intellectual bias that matter does not create matter or life is not created from non-living matter through random chemical processes, and that information is always the product of intelligence or a mind. Although this fundamental belief is a starting point, it does not impact the process of scientific inquiry. Someone with a bias toward intelligent design does not logically conclude that natural processes should not be studied, only that the two greatest mysteries in nature – spontaneous creation and phenomenon of life – have been answered.

The first step in understanding and dealing with a potential inhibiting bias is developing self-awareness that an inherent bias is actually present. We often develop views that are the product of our learning environment. It is not a self-indictment to have a bias. A bias becomes problematic whenever it hinders objectivity to protect closely held beliefs that cannot stand against scrutiny. When we hold biases up to examination, we cannot only identify flaws in a bias but also potentially strengthen our views by challenging them through independent fact-finding. What is difficult to comprehend, especially for a young adult or student, is that teachers and professors that are so often looked up to in the classroom are often guilty of guarding or seeking to confirm their own biases rather than challenging them in an academic environment.

Confirmation Bias

Confirmation bias has been defined as the "seeking or interpreting of evidence in ways that are partial to existing beliefs, expectations, or a hypothesis at hand."[15] Altering or ignoring evidence that is contrary to deeply held beliefs or expectations can be challenging. Concerning criminal cases, even experienced investigators must guard against fulfilling a confirmation bias when conducting complex investigations through clarification questions, follow-up interviews, and potential further analysis of physical evidence. If a prosecutor discovers exculpatory evidence, which points to the innocence of a defendant, case law has established that such evidence must be presented as such, even if it results in a prosecutor having to dismiss the criminal case altogether. This of course is a requirement of true justice and fairness. A criminal trial is designed to weigh allegations in a court of truth, ideally, where justice is blind, and the facts are weighed independently.

Scientists are just as susceptible to confirmation bias as anyone else even though they are typically viewed as intelligent, objective, and systematic in their approach to scientific inquiry.[16] This reality is that confirmation bias is existent within the scientific community and the "cult of science says" possesses the ability to promote or conclude false results from a study. Moreover, confirmation bias can especially be dominant when dealing with deeply held or emotional beliefs about a given topic. Even when confirmation bias creates problems of accuracy or validity in science, the popular belief would most likely hold to the view that these types of errors are a rare anomaly. Unfortunately, people within the scientific community acknowledge that such is not the case.

In a recent tell-tale book, *Rigor Mortis: How Sloppy Science Creates Worthless Cures, Crushes Hopes, and Wastes Billions*, award-winning science journalist Richard Harris reveals troubling realities within the scientific community. In one interview with a scientist, Harris was informed by a scientist that he interviewed that "most published scientific findings are false."[17] Harris' findings bring an astonishing report by someone who has been working in the scientific field for more than three decades. Such an alarming quote of course needs further validation. Other sources provide supporting documentation that "it is widely believed that most published scientific findings are false" and these numbers are followed by an awareness of the lack of accountability through quality peer review.[18]

Similarly, the non-profit organization, *Retraction Watch*, has more than 30,000 retracted articles in their database and recently shared that they are approaching 200 retracted Covid related articles from 2020.[19] Nowhere in recent times has the mantra "science says," been more used in the media, politics, and the workplace than with issues related to Covid safety and prevention. Retraction of research in the form of a publication in a peer-reviewed journal is among the most serious offenses that can occur within academia, either because of human error or academic misconduct. There appears to be a systemic issue with accountability about the publication of scientific research.

If there is to be a call for skepticism, it should be a call from within and for the scientific and academic community. The twentieth century has become a tale of two cities for the scientific community. In one venue, amazing discoveries launched our reach far into the darkest regions of space, as well as the magnificent depths of the human cell. However, in another venue, science and academia, propelled significantly by Darwinian evolution, have resulted in horrific atrocities and highly questionable conduct throughout the modern world. The strong have eliminated the weak in the name of advancement and morality has been erased by the conscience of the greater good.

Examining the Evidence: 🔍

This chapter examined the faulty claims of skepticism as virtuous because it is not holistically applied to a skeptics' belief system. Skepticism is only virtuous when applied without dominant blinders of personal or confirmation bias. It has also been determined that the great scientists of the scientific revolution were also men of faith and believed in a Creator, but that did not prevent them from engaging in scientific discoveries to search out the "how" questions. However, one of the most critical pieces of evidence in this chapter is that leading atheists have shared the logical result of a naturalistic worldview as one that does not pursue truth, only survival. When drawn to its logical conclusion, atheism is truly "an acid that burns through everything." If our brain is the product of mindless, unguided processes, it cannot be trusted to engage in logic, and, when it is, the results simply cannot be trusted when drawn to its natural conclusion.

A true skeptic will begin by addressing critical questions around a given topic. A true skeptic will address his or her own biases and seek to answer tough questions and not ignore evidence that brings an indictment on one's worldview. So, you, the reader, must decide what standard of evidence has been met? Is it more likely than not that there are serious intellectual arguments against atheism (or naturalism) as being a valid worldview or starting point by which to engage in critical thought about science? Is it more likely than not that both personal and confirmation bias is widespread in the academic community for both students and teachers or professors that prevents a genuine intellectual pursuit of truth?

"Do not be conformed to this world, but be transformed by the renewal of your mind, that by testing you may discern what is the will of God, what is good and acceptable and perfect."

Romans 12:2

2 Defining Your Worldview

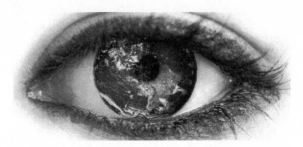

Defining a consistent worldview is essential for accurately interpreting or evaluating phenomena in the world around us. A worldview has been described as "one's total outlook on life, society, and its institutions."[1] Another definition that brings greater clarity is that a worldview is "a set of interrelated assumptions about the nature of the world."[2] A keyword to having an effective worldview is "interrelated." Everyone has a worldview, but not everyone has a worldview that is logically consistent in an interrelated way. Frequently, people grow up without paying attention to their worldview and therefore are unable to operate within their worldview consistently.

A consistent application means that one's interpretation of worldview principles affects other areas in an interrelated manner, like gears working in a mechanical application that move in a corresponding sequence. Some very intelligent people have a fractured, inconsistent worldview that is not relevant in their own life because it lacks a proper application on critical issues and often succumbs to personal bias or peer pressure. In a consistent, interrelated worldview, key assumptions in one area necessarily affect logical assumptions in other areas. However, too many go through life as if they were in an intellectual buffet line picking and choosing truth claims based on feeling instead of logic.

The difficulty sometimes arises when discussing issues within educational settings because too few students have developed a consistent worldview and, even more problematic, too few educators and professors have a consistent and coherent worldview themselves. It would be a significant mistake to assume that educators with the two or three letters after their name have established a broad knowledge base that interrelates key questions and issues consistently. Professors and educators often invest in research and develop expertise in their specific areas of interest that are usually limited in scope, but quite in-depth. Problems can arise whenever teachers or professors apply a limited worldview not only in their field of expertise but to all issues brought up in a classroom for discussion or in research by students.

There are at least four interrelated categories that should be covered in an adequate worldview: *Origin, Meaning, Morality,* and *Destiny.* These four foundational categories encompass the entire scope of perceptive reality and create the interpretive lens through which we view our world and the information we take in about the world for classification and assessment. Ultimately, it should be our worldview from which we speak on topics with authority and how they are related to other areas. As we frame intellectual concepts, we should either reject conclusions that force us outside of established frames of reference within our worldview about these key issues or reexamine our worldview altogether.

If you believe that human beings are created in God's image and likeness, as described in the Bible, then decisions about human beings related to dignity, rights, justice, and care should be made with the foundational understanding of the inherent value of people as God's creation. If you believe that human beings are just higher levels of animals with no spirit or soul, then that belief should hold consistency in personal decisions about meaning and morality. When it comes to worldviews, it is easy to take an *ala carte* approach to issues or topics, but it is logically inconsistent to break apart key, interrelated issues that address who we are, why we are here, what is right and wrong, and ultimately, what is our ultimate destiny as a species.

Origin

At the root of our existence rests the question of who we are and where we come from as human beings. Norman Geisler concluded that "the most important question a worldview answers is, "Where did we come from?"[3] The first of the four successive lenses through which we view the world must identify what it means to be a human being. The fundamental understanding of what it means to be a human being sets the standard for future interpretations within our worldview and our worldview must be consistent in its application as we move forward with other important questions in life. Questions about ethics and morality, as will be referenced later, are always asked within the context of what a human being does or does not do therefore those questions should logically begin with one's interpretation of what it means to be a human being.

Defining what it means to be a human involves an inherent assessment of the holistic value of human life. Looking at human value through our base chemical make-up, that is, all of the elements that make up the human body, our net worth is approximately six hundred U.S. dollars.[4] While a reasonable person would not ascribe such a devalued worth to a human being, there is still a stratified value placed on human beings based on a consistent interpretation of one's worldview. While an atheist with a naturalists or materialists worldview would most certainly argue against a monetary value of human life based only on chemical composition, they would not be able to logically affirm any comprehensive value of what it means to be a human regarding having eternal significance such as referring to the human soul or spirit.

A theistic (Christian) worldview, when consistent, holds to the inherent value of human beings as unique and created in the *Image of God*. Spirit, soul, and body make up a human being and it is the basis for any qualitative decision-making related to justice, dignity, and basic human rights. Again, consistency in this worldview is foundational and historical deviations, as frequently noted by atheists, will be addressed in chapter ten, which considers issues regarding the problem of evil. A consistent worldview involving humanity will offer two options: a divine design for purpose or the end-result of random variations by chance through natural, unguided processes that brought us to the level of sophisticated animals, but animals nonetheless.

Meaning

The American sage Mark Twain once wrote, "The two most important days in our life are the day we were born and the day we figure out why."[5] To atheists such as Richard Dawkins, Sam Harris, and the late Christopher Hitchens, their life has taken on meaning by vehemently opposing religion. Their book deals and speaking calendars have centered on debates and lectures about why religion is a force for evil in our world, a belief that was ingrained in them as a result of selected examples of religious-based evils in history. During an interview with National Public Radio (NPR), Dawkins identified his meaning in life as turning people toward secularism and evolution by stating that religion is, "one of the few things that's really strong enough to motivate people to do these terrible [acts of terrorism]."[6] Harris admits that he began writing his breakout book, *The End of Faith* the day after the terrorist attacks in America. Harris found meaning in what he was doing in his stand against religion.[7]

The logical contradiction with these atheists is that they are finding meaning in telling people, essentially, there is no meaning in life – the logical conclusion as one who is the product of random, unguided processes. Atheism advocates that we are not special and there is a series of quotes by Richard Dawkins, perhaps the most well-known advocate for evolution and naturalism, to come to that conclusion. Ironically, without God or religion, these atheists would have no real meaning in life as it relates to their compelling interest to free the world of religious conviction.

In a theistic worldview, meaning is primarily tied to who we are as God's creation and, more importantly, His image. This fact alone should give us meaning in life. Do we find meaning in our career, our service to others, and our family and friends? Absolutely! But when we are not yet in our career, or when we do not have a family, or when we are sometimes feeling alone, our status does not take away meaning in our life. Our comprehensive understanding of meaning is also found in our faith and our relationship with our Creator. It is a profound experience to understand true "meaning" when we possess an inherent value of human beings both within ourselves, as well as in those around us.

We also find meaning in caring for our planet, again referencing Genesis chapter one, Adam and Eve are given the mandate to care for God's creation. We as human beings are moved in awe of God's creation – breathtaking views of our planet and we absolutely lose ourselves over animals, especially our pets. Do atheists or Darwinian evolutionists ever wonder why we find such meaning and put forth so much time, money, and effort in caring for animals? It seems contradictory for humans with a genetic disposition for DNA propagation and biological advancement that we would invest so much time, effort, and money to care for lower animals.

A strict naturalist worldview that does not permit any theistic application cannot account for the innate awareness of who we are as well as the drive to care for others or God's creation as being inherently tied to meaning in our life. The only meaning Darwinian evolutionists should reference as an evolved species is propagating DNA. Lawrence Rifkin with *Scientific American* acknowledges the foundation of the naturalist worldview is that "Genetic evolution is the meaning of biologic life, in that it is the why and how of it, as well as the stock of future biological existence."[8] What Rifkin means by "biologic life" is a life that has no unique origin, specific meaning, or purpose other than to propagate future life. Life just came to be by chance and it will fade away as just another event that occurred on this lonely rock in space.

For atheists who subscribe to a naturalist worldview, meaning is tied up not in who we are, but rather our meaning is tied in with what we do at the most basic biological level. Whether raising cattle or raising children, the meaning of life in its most basic form is to propagate more and better DNA. Can someone who is a Darwinian evolutionist have an affinity for animals? Absolutely! Richard Dawkins is himself a zoologist by trade and Princeton Chair Peter Singer believes animals are just as valuable as human beings, in some cases, more so. However, evolutionists who subscribe to the premise that all of our motivations are inherently tied to our DNA cannot even be reconciled with a desire to care for others. There is a logical inconsistency within the foundational tenets of the naturalist worldview. This is a key area where the worldview of atheists breaks down in consistency because they want the foundational worldview of Darwinian evolution to be true, but they cannot live within that worldview consistently on many levels, especially one where *meaning* is part of our worldview analysis.

Morality

Consistency is rather elusive when linking origin with meaning within a naturalist or atheist worldview, but the application of morality completely falls off the hinges for a true Darwinian evolutionist. This fact will be elucidated in later chapters but finding philosophical continuity within a worldview that believes that we are merely an advanced biological system, whose chief end is to propagate new and better DNA, is well beyond the scope of moral foundation arguments. Philosopher Alvin Plantinga points out, "according to naturalistic evolutionary theory, human beings, their parts, and cognitive faculties arose by a blind, mindless, purposeless process such that these things were selected for solely in virtue of survival value and reproductive advantage."[9]

Survival value and reproductive advantage is hardly a sustainable approach to developing a moral framework by which to live or evaluate the actions of others. A frequent saying of Richard Dawkins is, "The universe we observe has precisely the properties we should expect if there is, at the bottom, no design, no purpose, no evil, no good, nothing but blind, pitiless indifference… DNA neither cares nor knows. DNA just is. And we dance to its music."[10] Dawkins is blatantly honest, but also blatantly inconsistent. The realization that Dawkins holds to this view of morality and also has a disdain for religion because it is, in his words, "evil," is quite the paradox. The charismatic Jim Jones who orchestrated the death of almost a thousand people as part of a religious cult in Guiana or terrorists who have murdered thousands in recent decades were, according to Dawkins, just "dancing to their DNA." What then is the issue with Dawkins assessing moral value statements about people like this in his books and during his frequent lectures to students?

People who ideologically identify with Dawkins seemingly have a fractured, inconsistent worldview because they cannot tie the ultimate mandate of survival to moral paradigms in society.

Dawkins himself has immense knowledge of biology and is a dedicated writer; his books have sold in the millions, but Richard Dawkins is a poor philosopher, a trait that is all too common with people who identify as atheists. It is very difficult to develop and consistently apply moral constructs in our world when you have a worldview that lacks cohesiveness and consistency on critical issues involving morality.

The only value an atheist has is whatever value an individual applies personally to a specific moral question, there is nothing or no one higher. To some people, Abraham Lincoln was a great leader, to other people, mobster Lucky Luciano, who brought different criminal organizations together to negotiate and work together for maximum illicit profit, was a great leader. The only standard or gauge for morality is an individual perspective because it is all relative and there can be no moral absolutes or high ground without an ultimate moral standard above the people or actions in question. An individual by him or herself who does not believe in absolute morality cannot argue on the grounds of morality. Most acknowledge that there is a moral compass within human beings that is distinct and not the product of evolution. C.S. Lewis came to this distinction as an atheist, and it resulted in his abandoning the utility of atheism.

C.S. Lewis, like Hitchens, Harris, and others, was intellectually born into atheism as a result of tragedy and suffering. Lewis had lost his mother to cancer when he was young, and, like so many other prominent atheists, had a father who was absent from his life, these events ultimately served to bolster his atheism.[11] Later, Lewis served in the British Army during World War I and experienced horrific trench warfare in the *Battle of the Somme*, where Lewis was severely injured and lost close friends in battle. However, it was initially the argument for a universal moral imperative in human interaction that ultimately led to Lewis' abandonment of atheism for theism. Lewis viewed, rather strongly, that there was evidence of a moral thread interwoven into the fabric of mankind that was *a priori* to cultural nuances or social learning.

Lewis's argument holds true today in the application of criminal justice. The American court system has included within case law words describing wrongful behavior that "shocks the conscience" as a result of being extremely unjust and that also demands a remedy by the court. Moreover, the courts use the standard of the conscience within a context of a "reasonable person" as it relates to interpreting human behavior. It would be safe to assume that when the *Richard Dawkins Foundation for Reason and Science* filed a civil lawsuit against a former employee that it was seeking remedy for an unjust act as to be determined by a reasonable person. In being consistent with Dawkins' worldview, however, the behavior of the employee might as well of been written by off Dawkins' foundation as his "merely dancing to his DNA."

Destiny

The concept of "destiny" is both abstract and metaphysical, but it has real application in our lives. So, why does destiny matter so much to humans? Why do we agonize over a loss and the thought of living for a relatively brief period and then dying? Could it be that what King Solomon wrote in Ecclesiastes 3:11, "That God has put eternity in the heart of man" is true? Or, is the concept of God or an afterlife just a human construct that was created because, as Stephen Hawking once said, "Man is afraid of the dark?" When Oxford Professor and Christian John Lennox was asked to respond to Hawking's claim, he light-heartedly replied, "Atheism is a fairy tale for those afraid of the light."[12] The light being referred to by Lennox could be understood as the central message of Christianity.

The Bible provides a thematic message for God's people. It begins with God calling his people out of Egypt, Exodus 6:7, "then I will take you as my people, and I will be your God...." These words are mentioned over thirty times throughout the Bible by prophets and Apostles and culminate with the end of time, Revelation 21:3, "And I heard a loud voice from the throne saying, "Behold! The tabernacle of God is among the people, and he will dwell among them. They shall be his people, and God himself will be among them." Upon closer examination what is amazing is the proclamation that *God will dwell among us*. God is coming to us because he is pursuing us and that is a love that defines our destiny.

Our destiny is in the presence of God for all eternity, in a new heaven, on a new earth, and with a new, glorified body. We will experience love as we have never known in an uncorrupted world in an uncorrupted body. Our destiny is not one of hope based on blind faith, but evidence-based faith that we are forever tied with Christ and his resurrection. You would think anyone, even an atheist, would be glad to hear such news, but the truth is that many people are atheists not because they don't have sufficient proof that God exists, but because they do not want proof that God exists. Their issue is not an issue of the mind, but an issue of a corrupted heart that despises its Creator.

There is no point for elaboration on a worldview that believes in no god and no life after death. The destiny of an atheist (naturalist or materialist), in his or her own words, is simply to cease to exist. It would be one thing if atheists approached the question of our origin, meaning, morality, and destiny, in a hopeful, inquisitive manner, but concluded, after thoroughly examining evidence, that there was no God. However, the presumptive belief in no God, no afterlife, and no supreme moral authority, typically rules the day in the atheist intellect and they are not only happy with that assessment but some are willing to argue such an assessment with full vigor.

Groupthink

Having a logically consistent worldview is critical to analyzing issues internally, but the realization is that external influences weigh heavily on one's worldview as well and, if a worldview lacks consistency, it also lacks resolve. The 1950s and 1960s experienced a series of groundbreaking experiments and theories on human behavior. Solomon Asch's *Conformity Experiment* was a key theory in understanding how people, in this case, students, respond to social conformity in decision-making in a learning environment. The result of the experiment was that three-quarters of the participants in the study gave a knowingly wrong answer when members of the control group were instructed to say the wrong answer beforehand to solicit conformity from students who were the target group of the study.

The factors that were found to influence conformity included that, (1) conformity tends to increase when more people are present, although there is a plateau in the effect, (2) conformity increases when the task becomes more difficult, one has to wonder if explaining the origin of all reality fits into the category of a "difficult task," and (3) conformity increases when members of the group are of a higher social status, e.g., more knowledgeable, powerful or influential.[13] These factors describe the context for almost any learning environment. The influential factors could be met by upperclassmen, or unfortunately, ideological professors seeking to propagate their opinions among influential students. A serious question must be considered, "How many young people of faith are walking away from an intellectual belief in God because they are conforming to people who they perceive as more intelligent or having a higher status, not because of ground-breaking evidence or logical conclusions?"

General George Patton once said, "If everyone is thinking alike, then somebody isn't thinking."[14] Having served on an Army General's Staff for more than four years, I can quickly identify the urgency of Patton's quote. A staff function for any level of command is to identify weaknesses and vulnerabilities to operations and strategy. The effective staff works through differences to come up with realistic solutions to problems and they do not achieve this result from "groupthink." They develop responses and estimates based on the most reliable information (or evidence) available, and, sometimes, they have to tell a commander that he or she is incorrect in their assumptions.

There is extreme value in collaboration, but there is no virtue to quiet conformity in a classroom setting on important issues, especially when evidence or research speaks to differences in the consensus. Since 2020, 140 years after Darwin died, evolutionary scientists have made a bold statement that there was "no proof" for Darwin's theories of evolution.[15] Now that is a statement, especially when reported by Darwinian evolutionists, that will stymie groupthink on a consensus for evolution. Of course, they would argue that there is overwhelming evidence for Darwinian evolution, but again, research calls that assertion into question as will be demonstrated in the coming chapters.

Examining the Evidence:

Many of our conclusions in life, and in academia, are based on worldviews and biases that must challenge for internal consistency, but rarely are in actuality. Framing a worldview that enables consistency requires definitive understandings about our origin, meaning, morality, and ultimate destiny as human beings. When our origin, meaning, morality, and destiny are defined by a biological drive to only enhance our DNA the ability to maintain logical consistency on important issues becomes very difficult for even the most strident atheist. This reality is demonstrated in everyday interactions with people in our lives as well as within academia.

Do we love our children because there is something special about them or primarily because they are merely carrying on our DNA? The same question holds true with growing a family, do we marry someone we are biologically attracted to to propagate our DNA or is there something more to this thing we call "love?" What should a Darwinian evolutionist like Richard Dawkins, who criticizes religion for being "homophobic,"[16] say to same-sex couples who either cannot or do not want to propagate their DNA? If our underlying evolutionary drive is only to propagate our DNA then people who do not wish to propagate DNA, for whatever reason, must have something innately wrong with them from an evolutionary standpoint.

The evidence is overwhelmingly in support of a worldview that speaks to our origin, meaning, morality, and destiny as being more than a biological drive to preserve, enhance, and propagate our DNA. We are not merely beings innately driven to preserve our DNA because we know that sacrifice is among the highest virtues. In 2007 a twenty-year-old *New York Film Academy* student was standing in the subway when he had a seizure and collapsed on the railway tracks as a subway train was speeding towards him. In an instant, Wesley Autrey, a construction worker and Navy Veteran, leaped onto the helpless student convulsing on the tracks to protect him from being killed.[17] Autrey not only instinctively put his own life at risk, but his two daughters were with him and were at risk of seeing their father killed.

Another amazing inherent reality within our nature is that we experience a greater sense of fulfillment when we serve other human beings. One of my collateral duties in the Army is serving as a Master Resilience Instructor to help Soldiers overcome the mental stress of serving in combat or arduous duty. My certification came through an intensive certification process that was developed and written at the University of Pennsylvania under the supervision of Dr. Martin Seligman, former president of the

American Psychological Association and the author of the book I had initially read titled *Authentic Happiness*.

In his book, Seligman references research that juxtaposes the experience of people doing what they loved doing with that of volunteering to help someone or some organization. The results that Seligman reports reflect an overwhelming greater sense of happiness in positive emotion in serving others than even doing the things that we love doing the most.[16] Our feeling of meaning and purpose increases dramatically whenever we invest in helping others, not selfishly pondering the quality or future of our DNA or even just engaging in a hobby.

"See to it that there is no one who takes you captive through philosophy and empty deception in accordance with human tradition, in accordance with the elementary principles of the world, rather than in accordance with Christ."

Colossians 2:8

3   Revolution for Evolution

On November 24, 1859, the book *On the Origin of Species: By Means of Natural Selection, or the Preservation of Favoured Races in the Struggle for Life* was published by Charles Darwin. Darwin's theory is held up by two distinct pillars: random mutation occurs with variations within species and nature decides which mutations will survive and which ones will not.[1] It is very doubtful that Darwin was aware of the social, cultural, and historical impact his theory would have throughout the modern world when he started to pen his book. Darwin was not the first to consider evolution, but he would launch a naturalistic movement that would sweep across western civilization and ultimately change the direction and study of biology.[2]

However, biology was not the only discipline that applied his theory. Darwinian evolution impacted every aspect of academia and permeated American thought everywhere.[3] Darwinian evolution also included influences on theological interpretations in divinity studies as well as sermons of this era as a progression of naturalism. A few decades before Darwin, a theological movement sprung up out of the Enlightenment that began to strip away supernatural tenets from explanations about our world. Modernism had dawned and Darwin became a natural fit as described by Richard Dawkins who concludes, "Darwin made it possible to be an intellectually fulfilled atheist."[4] Darwinian evolution seemed to now be the universal theory for how the world, and potentially the universe, operated.

The rapid development of Darwinian evolution resulted

in aftershocks throughout society in a collective embrace of evolutionary theory as a scientific fact that is still felt today. The validity of Darwinian evolution was promoted through naturalistic worldviews as well as the public perception that was shaped within academia. One would be hard-pressed to find the collective solidarity of evolution as fact more than theory than in the U.S. court system where there have been ten distinct court rulings in America that have prohibited evolution from being challenged in the classroom with competing theories and those judicial opinions have even restricted teachers from providing disclaimers on problems or weaknesses of Darwinian evolution to students.[5]

The cultural view is pushed that in American academia, and western thought in general, intelligent people embrace Darwinism as the explanation for life on earth. Conversely, only the unsophisticated embrace the idea or belief system that God or some form of an intelligent designer is the causal agent in our universe. Somewhat surprisingly, even the highest office within the Catholic Church embraces Darwinian evolution as both consistent with the creation story of Scripture and, from the words of Pope John Paul II, "evolution is more than a hypothesis."[6] While most people of faith, including those within the Catholic community, may not subscribe to Darwinian evolution, it is the authority behind the Catholic Church that lends credibility to this theory within some religious circles. Furthermore, Finnish scientist Matti Leisola asserts that in his home country the Lutheran church has aligned with universities and scientists in what he calls, "a united front in defense of Darwinian evolution by reassuring the public that the theory of evolution has been convincingly proved."[7]

The effects of putting humanity at the apex of a new moral paradigm with evolution at its base have proven catastrophic and its historical impact has been extremely controversial when examined through a critical lens. With Darwinian evolution serving as the torchbearer for human advancement in multiple disciplines, the betterment of humanity had been placed largely in the hands of scientists. The problem with this approach is that science is a unique discipline that is not compatible when trying to evaluate or measure anything to do with moral agency. New atheist Sam Harris acknowledges the incompatibility of science with moral agency as he acknowledges, "Science is about facts, not norms; it might tell us how we are, but it couldn't tell us what is wrong with how we are. There couldn't be a science of the human condition."[8]

The moral foundations of science arrive outside of the discipline of science. Science, in its amazing capacity, can provide a vaccine for a disease, but it will not inform anyone as to who should get the vaccine, that decision must come outside of science. History has revealed that when scientific inquiry extends to moral mandates the result can be less than desirable and even tragic. What's even more problematic is that humanity struggles to overcome or learn the failures when science and morality are intertwined in policies or social norms.

Just over a decade after publishing his seminal work on evolution, Darwin turned his focus specifically on human evolution in the *Descent of Man and Selection in Relation to Sex*. Darwin's goal was threefold. First, he sought to clarify his theory that mankind descended from primates. Second, Darwin wanted to address human development, and third, distinguish between the different races of men.[9] Darwin's most recent work also became his most controversial. Unlike his first work, *Descent* was not embraced with the fanfare that he experienced in *Origin*. Darwin took the liberty to express the intellectual dominance of males over females as well as the categorization of different ethnic groups as correspondingly being on different levels of evolutionary development.[10] While Darwin had made references to man's evolving from lower animals in his original work, the focused attention of his most recent efforts in correlating man with monkeys led not only to his name being in print, but his image caricatured as a primate in publications critical of his theory.

Darwin's most recent work may have drawn some criticism, even laughter, but the inherent substance of Darwin's theory was still solidified and moving forward within academia and influencing people in power. Whereas references between the intellectual gaps between men and women received obvious pushback from at least half the population, Darwin's classification of individuals with developmental disabilities had a more congenial response. Darwin argued that "idiots," as people with intellectual disabilities were often referred to in that era, were more directly connected to primates and that their status as the lowest of our species could reveal the earliest stages of human evolution.[11] Darwin also believed that these "idiots" could do what the fossil record could not, and that was to provide the "missing link" between species on the evolutionary ladder in that the mentally disabled represented the lowest rung.[12]

In *Descent*, Darwin gives a summary analysis of how society should deal with the physically and mentally weak,

"With savages, the weak in body or mind are soon eliminated; and those that survive commonly exhibit a vigorous state of health. We civilized men, on the other hand, do our utmost to check the process of elimination; we build asylums for the imbecile, the maimed, and the sick; we institute poor-laws, and our medical men exert their utmost skill to save the life of everyone to the last moment. There is reason to believe that vaccination has preserved thousands, who from a weak constitution would formerly have succumbed to smallpox. Thus, the weak members of civilized societies propagate their kind. No one who has attended to the breeding of domestic animals will doubt that this must be highly injurious to the

race of man. It is surprising how soon a want of care or care wrongly directed, leads to the degeneration of a domestic race; but excepting in the case of man himself, hardly any one is so ignorant as to allow his worst animals to breed."[13]

When understanding Darwin's view on the sick and the feeble, it is surprising to learn that Darwin himself suffered from moderate to extreme maladies all of his adult life, ultimately dying from Crohn's disease at the age of 73.[14] Darwin had been treated by twenty different physicians in search of relief from digestive, skin, and other health problems, including depression, but his actual diagnosis, based on symptomatology remains a mystery with only speculation as to the underlying cause of his suffering from poor health.[15] What we do know is that Darwin did not relent on his opinion of others in society who were genetically disposed to illnesses and weakness and there was a scientific mandate to prevent such people from intermingling in society or to propagate those weaknesses through breeding.

Eugenics

Francis Galton, a cousin to Darwin, took Darwinian evolution to its next logical step, which was facilitating natural selection through the intentional manipulation of hereditary strengths and weaknesses within the human species. Eugenics or the study of "good genes," has been defined as the science of improving the human race by scientific control of breeding.[16] The sweeping developments and application of Darwinian evolution, as well as its acceptance by leaders in both academia and society, resulted in a new-found authority, backed by the science of eugenics, to forcibly sterilize "feeble-minded" girls and categorize individuals as unfit to reproduce.

In 1907 the state of Indiana became the first government to pass eugenics laws with involuntary sterilizations targeting "confirmed criminals, idiots, imbeciles and rapists."[17] Some Criminologists in academia proposed theories of criminal behavior to involve atavistic tendencies on the assumption that certain characteristics such as facial features were predictors of criminal behavior because they displayed atavistic features and were evolutionarily backward.[18] The danger of this approach to crime in society is that labeling individuals as having atavistic traits categorize them differently than other individuals and potentially compromises constitutional requirements of equal treatment under the law.

The eugenics movement in the United States also attracted pre-WW2 German scholars and scientists and there was significant academic collaboration in eugenics studies between the two countries. Edwin Black's *War Against the Weak and America's Campaign to Create a Master Race* draws a direct correlation between the eugenics movement in the United States and Nazi Germany. Social icon, author, and nurse Margaret Sanger, who has a dedicated exhibit in the Smithsonian Museum, was a strong advocate for forced sterilization and segregation of an estimated fifteen to twenty million Americans because of perceived racial impurities.[19] Sanger was also the founder of *Planned Parenthood*, and it was not until July 2020 that the Manhattan Planned Parenthood office finally removed Sanger's name as a result of her "harmful connections to the eugenics movement."[20]

In the late 1920s, the U.S. Supreme Court finally intervened in these horrific practices and overturned eugenics laws related to forced sterilization. However, the damage had been done with government-mandated actions against the "unfit" and Nazi Germany now had the blueprint for their version of a "master race" void of "less desirables." While Germany's Second Reich had already been involved in genocide in West Africa based on social Darwinian principles, the first genocide of the twentieth century, its population had been unscathed by eugenics laws. The first significant step for Germany to eliminate undesirable people within its borders came in 1933 with the passing of the *"Law for the Prevention of Hereditarily Diseased Offspring."* Approximately five years later a more aggressive measure was enacted called the T4 program or *Action T4.*

The T4 program, named for the address of the office responsible for overseeing the operation, involved physicians screening patients to be "euthanized" and it was Germany's first mass murder as 300,000 children, women, and men gassed to death.[21] The application of T4 resulted in an effective and efficient means of murder and was later used in death camps across Nazi-occupied Europe to kill "undesirables" by the millions. However, it also desensitized many who would take part in this mass medical malpractice as a solution to the greater good. Darwinian evolution provided a pathway for humanity to evolve physically through a moral mandate of the greater good.

In his book *From Darwin to Hitler: Evolutionary Ethics, Eugenics, and Racism in Germany,* Richard Weikart argues that the Nazi justification for evolutionary "fitness" was the ultimate measure of morality.[22] Just as there was a Darwinian evolutionary tree that proposed that mankind had evolved from animalistic roots down from a single-cell organism, there was also a eugenics tree, drafted by Galton, with its deepest roots grafted into evolutionary theory. Eugenicists believed that mankind could eliminate undesirable traits which would lead to a race of people who were pristine in evolutionary development. However, for many eugenicists, pristine genetics also included the model typology, as white, Anglo-Saxons because this ethnic group had evolved furthest from their prehistoric biological ancestors, knuckle-dragging primates.

Ideas Have Consequences

The Nuremberg trials did not fully develop the role of evolutionary thought and eugenics as part of the *mens rea* (intent) of the criminal intent of the Nazi criminals, only the *modus operandi*. In his book, *The Nazi Doctors*, Psychiatrist Robert Jay Lifton references his work interviewing Nazi doctors. When asked by a victim of the holocaust, "Were they beasts?" Lipton replied, "They were and are men... their behavior was a product of human ingenuity and cruelty. Neither brilliant, nor stupid, neither inherently evil nor particularly ethically sensitive, they were by no means the demonic figures—sadistic, fanatic, lusting to kill—people have often thought of them to be." To which the holocaust survivor responded, "But it is demonic, that they were not demonic."[23]

The term "Nazi" gets thrown around a lot as the ultimate insult related to allegations of someone's moral turpitude, especially by angry activists. However, the evils carried out in Nazi Germany, according to the work of Lifton, have more normalized roots as a result of Darwinian evolution. Holocaust survivor and Psychiatrist Viktor Frankl provided a heuristic insight when he wrote, "I am absolutely convinced that the gas chambers of Auschwitz, Treblinka, and Maidanek were ultimately prepared not in some Ministry or office in Berlin, but rather at the desks and lecture halls of nihilistic scientists and philosophers."[24] Atheism is, in part, a product of nihilism because there were or are no absolutes. This worldview became normalized to varying degrees under Darwinian evolution.

The horrific acts of systematic murder during the holocaust were being carried out by relatively normal people – women and men of various age groups and backgrounds within Germany. From an evolutionary perspective, this has to be taken under some consideration. Do we not have an intellectual "March of Progress?" Were these acts the result of large numbers of people being tricked or fooled into processing babies, children, women, and men into death camps for extermination or torturous medical experimentation? If history offers any consolation, it would be that we as a human species have learned from mistakes of the past and are now better suited through awareness to stop horrific events centered on dehumanization from developing. Or are we?

In the 1950s the now-infamous Stanley Milgram experiment of Yale University was completed as an inquiry into a theory related to behavior by WWII-era Germans leading up to and during the holocaust. His theory, as well as published research work such as that of Robert Lifton, give significant weight to the argument that well-intended human beings can commit horrific acts if there is an authority figure present, the act is legal or sanctioned, and there is some good that could come out of the act. For the Milgram experiment, the good was scientific inquiry and the need to understand more about how humans recall memory. The authority figure was the professor in the lab coat providing guidance and instruction, he was also a channel to blame if anything bad happened. In the experiment, 65% of the participants administered, "lethal levels of electric shock" to the unknown person behind the wall, even to the simulated sound of horrific screams and cries to stop the electric shocks.[25]

However, even more alarming is that leading up to and during the holocaust, physicians, of whom more than half practicing in Germany joined the Nazi party and actually surpassed party enrollments of all other professions, were spearheading the effort to torture and murder people."[26] In addition to physicians, there were nurses, assistants, drivers, administrators, guards, and others who played a direct role in the mass murder of millions of people simply for being deemed genetically inferior. Thirty years before *T4* the citizenry was outraged that their army was engaging in genocide in West Africa and now horrific acts were taking place in their own country against their own citizenry in the name of science and medicine.

The influence of Darwinian evolution and twentieth-century eugenics has immeasurable historical relevance within academia. During this time scientific progress was at the forefront in America and Germany. Some evolutionists and eugenicists in America even had academic buildings and schools named after them because of their work in eugenics. The eugenics movement continued in America, only stopping after a heightened awakening by the *Third Reich* after WW2 had ended.[27] Today, horrific practices such as partial-birth abortion seemingly meet all three tenets – a person does not want the baby, it's legal to murder a baby, in most cases regardless of fetal development, it is "good" that an unwanted baby is not brought in the world.

In a recent comment, U.S. Supreme Court Justice Sonia Sotomayor drew broad criticism after comparing fetal movements including recoiling from the pain of being dismembered in the womb to the physiological reaction of a brain-dead person to argue that a fetus was not a sentient being.[28] Such a statement by an intelligent legal analyst brings to the forefront the importance of not only having academic smarts but a systematic and cogent worldview. This Supreme Court Justice, like many others, is apparently incapable of critically analyzing arguments and evidence because of a staunch pro-choice personal opinion, an a priori approach to issues of socio-political relevance. Of course, the Supreme Court Justice is simply parroting the pro-choice movement and the result of this systematic practice finds the surfacing of an old philosophy that was thought to have ended after WW2, *Lebensunwertes Leben* or "Life Unworthy of Life."

The true number of atrocities that have been committed against people because of a worldview that believes that there is nothing significant about humanity for whatever reason will never be known. The struggle for human dignity spans from the battlefield to the courts and the dangers of this is not only demonstrated in history but through experiments and psychological theory. The relative ease by which human dignity is stripped away from a person (or fetus) is alarming but Darwinian evolution has dulled the collective senses to the horrific practices of dehumanization in different contexts.

It has been argued that Darwinian evolution provided the answers that atheists desperately wanted to counter the claims of God. Evolution has evolved into a faith system for the "faithless." Those who live under the Darwinian tree can see no light or special status for humanity. The mind of a naturalist or scientific materialist can apparently imagine any wonderful concept or theory to answer complex problems except one involving a supernatural or intelligent being outside of time and matter. Atheists can mentally assent to complex life just spontaneously appearing in primordial soup or an eternal universe that ultimately created them, but they cannot image or even hypothesize an eternal Creator... or at least they refuse to.

Examining the Evidence: 🔍

The history and developments of Darwinian evolution have been problematic over the past century. Evolution, more than any other belief system, has been the foundation of horrific evils in society whether that is forced sterilization in the United States or genocide on different continents. Just as problematic, is that leaders in governments as well as physicians, or those with a sworn oath to "do no harm," have been guilty of carrying out some of history's most brutal acts of violence against some of the most helpless victims in the name of science. In Germany, the term was "Life Unworthy of Life," in America other titles have been used to dehumanize others such as idiot or imbecilic, but there are many more that have been used to justify violence including *fetus.*

In the 150 years of Darwinian evolution, we can better understand human health and disease, but again, the concepts of evolution were around before Darwin published *Origin.* Evolutionary scientists may argue that "the key principles of evolutionary medicine are that selection acts on fitness, not health or longevity...."[28] However, the ambiguity of Darwinian evolution is that fitness equals survival, but the fact that one survives, according to Darwinists, equals one's level of fitness. Such circular arguments are a tautology or, saying the same thing twice in different words. Again, in addition to the failure to substantively define "natural selection," the words "survival" and "fit" are essentially the same thing said differently. Such ambiguity is the foundation for problems within the scientific community, especially in publications and within academia in general when they are not clearly and distinctly defined.

Ambiguity is dangerous in the world of science or moral calculation because these positions are dominated by people of influence and power. A strong, consistent worldview that accurately defines human beings makes it very difficult to navigate through any social or political system that labels people of any condition or level of development as anything but "human." To say with confidence that the human species is not capable of repeating the horrors of its past is putting too much confidence and assurance in the human condition.

"The heart is more deceitful than all else and desperately sick: who can understand it?"

Jeremiah 17:9

4   Evolution: Flaws & Faith

Just as the history of Darwinian evolution is troublesome, so too is the modern-day application of evolutionary theory within the scientific community. When challenged about the weaknesses of Darwinian evolution, Eugenie Scott, former Director for the National Center for Science Education, replied, "There are no weaknesses in evolution."[1] Any critical thinker should follow up that assertion based on gaps in knowledge within the scientific establishment concerning evolution. Moreover, evidence that contradicts Darwinian evolution should be considered sufficient to classify as a "weakness" within the theory itself.

There is no doubt that species change over time, as Darwin noted by the Galapagos finch beak getting longer in winter months. However, Darwin's theory is not only that species evolve within species, but that all life on earth evolved from a single cell organism and evolved from natural selection. What many scientists are most likely not aware of is that this was a belief that Darwin had held approximately twenty years before his five-year trip to the Galapagos. However, Darwin had no evidence from an observation or a forensic vantage point to frame or support such a theory during the initial or even in the five follow-on editions of his book, *On the Origin of Species.*

Although the halls of academia seemingly have unlimited praise and scientific support for Darwinian evolution, there are plenty of opportunities for critical inquiry into the weaknesses of this theory. The academic and scientific community is quick to reference any opposition to Darwinian evolution as ignorance or at best, conjecture. Richard Dawkins gives a scathing rebuke of anyone who would question Darwinian evolution by saying, "It is absolutely safe to say that if you meet somebody who claims not to believe in evolution, that person is ignorant, stupid or insane (or wicked, but I'd rather not consider that)."[2] Dawkins' consideration of someone who does not believe in evolution as being "wicked," is a moral statement and such a statement by a materialist is in itself contradictory. That is not saying atheists cannot be moral people, but they have difficulty assigning moral blame to others where there is "no absolute moral standard," although Dawkins might consider science to be that standard, Einstein would most likely disagree with him if that were the case based on his assertions of morality and science.

The question should be asked regarding any inquiry into Darwinian evolution, "Are there weaknesses in Darwinian evolution which state that species change into new species over time as a result of random, unguided processes?" Charles Darwin was very honest about the weaknesses in his theory. It begs the question, "Did Eugenie Scott read Darwin's collective work when she proclaimed that evolution has no weaknesses?" Darwin's personal correspondence is revealing about his own struggles with his theory as well as his expressions of hope or faith that one day the answers to these problems and doubts would be provided – to date, the answers that Darwin hoped would be provided to fill problems and gaps within his theory are still not empirically answered.

In his book "On the Origin of Life," Darwin did not even attempt to develop a theory of how the origin of life came to be. It is like the theory of Darwinian evolution begins at "Chapter 2." Ernst Haeckel called Darwin's failure to address the origin of life within a simple cell the "chief defect of his theory."[3] Darwin did make a brief reference to an idea that is quite similar to what is found in today's textbooks, but Darwin's reference to the origin of life was fleeting and provided no insight for readers. Individuals who embrace Darwin's theory as a holistic explanation for life simply have to tie the origin of life in with the theory of the evolution of life in hopes that one day an answer to the actual origin of life will be answered. As for now, Darwinian evolutionists refer to the antiquated origin of life experiments to bolster their confidence that one day this elusive answer to the question of how life emerged from non-living matter will be provided by science and thereby fill in significant evidentiary gaps in the theory.

The Cambrian explosion

The most significant problem with Darwin's theory, according to Darwin, was that he could not account for the fossil finds in what has been coined the "Cambrian explosion." The Cambrian explosion can be defined as "the sudden and explosive diversification of life forms at the early Cambrian period as documented in the fossil record."[4] The Cambrian explosion has been referred to as "Evolution's Big Bang." Darwin theorized that life began in the Cambrian era and yet all of the readily available fossilized animal body plants are found together in this geological time capsule with complex eyes and multi-component body parts. These complex life forms did not have time to evolve in this era, but Darwin's theory concluded they evolved gradually in the animal phyla.[5] Even Richard Dawkins commented, "It's as though they were just planted there with no evolutionary history."[6]

Darwin did not attempt to conceal or minimize the impact of what the Cambrian discovery meant to his theory. To Darwin's credit, he called out the seriousness of this problem and wrote in *Origin*, that [the Cambrian discovery] was a serious problem which "at present must remain inexplicable; and may be truly urged as a valid argument against the views here entertained."[7] Those views, of course, were that of the evolutionary tree suggested by Darwin in that all animals ascended from one common ancestor. The

Cambrian fossil evidence found in China and Canada remains just as inexplicable today for evolutionists as it was when *Origin* was printed.

James Valentin, one of the scientists involved with modern-day Cambrian research, said of the discovery, "the record that we have is not very supportive of models that posit a long period of the evolution of metazoan phyla before the Cambrian period."[8] The collective response from hard-core Darwinian evolutionists was simply that something must have happened to the pre-Cambrian fossils, after all, they were soft-shell. However, pre-Cambrian era fossil finds in Canada include jellyfish, like the ones in our oceans today, algae, and other soft-shell phyla well preserved in the fossil record. These fossils show that the soft-shell hypothesis does not provide a valid response to the missing fossils that would pre-date the Cambrian era fossils.

Another problem for Darwin's theory in the Cambrian explosion was that the fossil record indicated that *Darwin's Tree* showing graduate change within species should be inverted. Darwin believed that animals evolved from the bottom up, the most significant differences in animal phyla being at the top. J.Y. Chen provides some extra commentary to clarify "Darwin's tree being inverted" in that, "The new phyla make their start in the early days, instead of coming at the top".[9] In other words, complex creatures are at the bottom and variations migrate up through the fossil record. The result of the significant find resulted in the conclusion of one paleontologist, "I think the Cambrian explosion is going to tell us something different about evolution, in the sense that it's not the same story that we have always been taught." Modern analysis of the fossil records brings to light more key evidence against Darwin's theory that all life evolved from a single organism, but there is no avenue by which to introduce paradigm-shifting thought on Darwinian evolution and this is itself a substantial weakness.

In 1999 Dr. J.Y. Chen, a leading paleontologist on the

Cambrian explosion, gave a presentation at the University of Washington on the Cambrian research and mentioned *Darwin's Tree* seemingly being inverted based on the fossil record. He was later asked during a Q&A session by a professor at the university about being concerned with questioning Darwin and living in a communist country. Dr. Chen replied, "In China, you can question Darwin, but not the government. In America, you can question the government, but not Darwin."[11] It is dreadfully revealing that a scientist from a very strict communist country, which often has a tight grip on individual expression of ideas, is able to contrast his country's freedom of academic expression with that of the United States to bring a contrast of true intellectual and academic freedom.

Mind vs. Matter

In 1965, there was a popular artist's illustration for *Time* magazine labeled, "The March of Progress" illustrating the evolution of *Homo sapiens* in line all the way down to chimpanzees. The illustration on the cover of *Time* became very popular as it captured the evolution of humanity as *Homo sapiens* who walked in front of Cro-Magnon Man who, in turn, walked in front of Neanderthal and the line continued to descend more than a dozen species down to knuckle-dragging primates. Modern Darwinian evolutionists themselves do not subscribe to this evolutionary lineage. However, it was acknowledged how useful the artistic concept was in propagating the theory of Darwinian evolution into mainstream culture[12]

Darwin's theory, that man descended from primates, has significant relevance today based specifically on a doubt that he wrote to William Graham about on July 3, 1881. Darwin's realization of what it meant to be evolved from lower animals was brought to a logical conclusion as he expressed his concern to Graham in what has been coined as "Darwin's Horrid Doubt,"

> "But then with me the horrid doubt always arises whether the convictions of man's mind, which has been developed from the mind of the lower animals, are of any value or at all trustworthy. Would anyone trust in the convictions of a monkey's mind, if there are any convictions in such a mind?"[13]

Darwin's candid honesty should be shared by so many who revere him as an icon within the scientific community. In realizing the weight of this reality in his theory, and his assertion that humans evolved from primates, Darwin asked a legitimate question that should be asked by all who strongly hold to Darwinian evolution. Oxford mathematician Dr. John Lennox has frequently asked in public forums in response to Darwin's doubt, "Would you buy a computer that was the product of mindless, unguided processes?"[14] Scientists who believe in materialistic reductionism, that all that exists is matter and energy, fail to fully realize that they are making that conclusion with a brain that is the end-product of mindless-unguided processes.

Atheists who hold a naturalist or materialist view have been quick to refer to the mental processes, experiences, and reactions as strictly a product of the brain. There is no room for a metaphysical concept of a "mind" in their worldview. While the contrast of the two may cause some to question the logic of such a distinction, it is consistent with an evolutionary worldview. If we are the product of mindless, unguided processes that have evolved from a single-cell organism brought to life by chance in a puddle of primordial ooze then there is nothing special about anything that takes place with the biological realm of our brain. However, Darwin's doubt becomes even more problematic for the dedicated materialists as scientists have made amazing discoveries concerning what we know about how people think and function intellectually.

While some might argue that this problem is merely philosophical, it is strongly embedded in the study of neuroscience and is categorized as "the mind-brain problem," which has been described as "one of the most fundamental philosophical and scientific questions that psychiatry faces."[15] Edmund Rolls (2013) of the Oxford Centre for Computational Neuroscience, states of the analogy between mind and brain, "this does leave some 'hard' problems, such as the problem of phenomenal consciousness... one must recognize that there is still somewhat of a gap in our understanding of events in the brain and the subjective experiences that may accompany them."[16] Scientists simply cannot explain with precise detail what "consciousness" is and many neuroscientists do hold a contrast between the brain and the mind. However, the gap in understanding still does not prevent Darwinian naturalists from incorporating convenient truths about the brain and the mind that are not consistent with evidence from within the scientific community.

The F---- Word

Darwinian evolutionary scientists like Richard Dawkins criticize people who believe in God or a Creator as living a life based on *faith* whereas scientists have *facts* as the foundation for their worldview. However, scientists routinely exercise faith, not only to bridge the identified gaps in Darwinian evolution but in their scientific method as well. When a scientist must rely on an assumption that she or he cannot prove through scientific methods, that person is relying on a belief system that is defined as faith. Moreover, faith is something scientists not only use in their field, but it is also something that they bring into their field. Nobel Prize winner George Klein wrote in *The Atheist in the Holy City: Encounters and Reflections,* "I am not an agnostic. I am an atheist. My attitude is not based on science, but rather on faith... The absence of a Creator, the non-existence of God is my childhood faith, my adult belief, unshakable and holy."[17]

The Pew Research Center acknowledges that Darwinian evolution is widely accepted by all but a few scientists and that the public's reservations for accepting Darwinian evolution "lie with the theological implications of evolutionary thinking."[18] The logical assumption from *Pew,* and other data, is that scientists view an intellectual schism between belief in God and scientific inquiry, and to entertain anything but a naturalist or materialist approach to science is both inappropriate and widely unaccepted within the scientific community. This of course is a preconceived belief system that guides scientific inquiry and is not a product of its methodology.

The view is that by eliminating any direct reference of the supernatural operating within the natural world, science is eliminating the concept of faith. However, scientists who bring assumptions that there is no god, only matter and energy, into their approach to scientific inquiry still exhibit some measure of faith that they are correct in their assumptions. Doors that lead to anything other than the appearance of design or intelligence are boarded shut through their own *a priori* beliefs, not because "science" leads to that conclusion. To this end, naturalism, or scientific materialism, often bolstered by Darwinian evolution, is a belief system that accommodates atheists through faith. Furthermore, with scientific discoveries such as the Cambrian explosion directly opposing Darwinian evolutionary theory, it takes remarkable faith for naturalists to ignore overwhelming evidence of design in creation. Unfortunately, atheists who have a naturalist worldview are not only blind to their application of faith, but they vehemently attack anyone who uses reasonable faith to come to conclusions about intelligence or creation, even when those conclusions are based on evidence including a combination of Scripture, history, personal experiences, and yes, science.

There is a common mantra among the scientific community, especially in naturalist or atheistic circles, that "science says…" and they use this verbiage to intimidate anyone who would question their methodology or conclusions. *Darwin's Tree* should have been chopped down immediately after it was planted in the minds of nineteenth-century scientists. Although its roots are now exposed, and the leaves are starting to fall, individuals still cling to this tree and believe, or have faith, that one-day science will come to their rescue. Scientists have faith that "science" will fill the extreme gaps in Darwinian theory to support a strict naturalist worldview. However, as scientific inquiry uncovers more and more of the amazing complexity of life and the origins of our universe, the more revealing it is that there is an intelligence and a mind behind it all.

Examining the Evidence: 🔍

Darwinian evolution was born into gaps and inconsistencies related to the fossil record and, just as importantly, Darwin's realization that if we are simply organisms evolved from lower life forms, how could we put trust and confidence in our mind. Darwin had faith that the gaps or inconsistencies in the fossil record would one day be solved as he promoted his theory and his book. He also held out that one-day science would one day cogently speak to the origin of life. It is quite ironic that Darwin's book "On the Origin of Species," does not even speak to the origin of life.

Scientists in the field of paleontology have made some amazing discoveries that refute Darwin's theory. There is simply no evidence that all life evolved upward on an evolutionary tree, but the response has been silent from within academia and scientific media has been complicit in the suppression of this fact. Not only is Darwinian evolution refuted by fossil evidence, but it is turned upside down. The facts of the evidence speak to the root cause of the problem in that changes to Darwinian evolution would require a glacial shift within institutions like the National Academy of Sciences for there to be any movement on the facts behind Darwinian evolution. So, for now, scientists will have to take their worldview on faith instead of facts, but there is no evidence of that happening anytime soon.

"For we did not follow cleverly devised tales when we made known to you the power and coming of our Lord Jesus Christ, but we were eyewitnesses of His majesty."
2 Peter 1:16

5 Scientism

Scientism is the belief that the hard sciences and their methods of inquiry, such as chemistry, biology, physics, and astronomy, provide the only true means to attain knowledge.[1] There are a couple of problems with this declaration. First, saying that science is the only way to truth is a statement of philosophy, not a statement of science, so, when drawn to its logical conclusion, the claim proves itself untrue. Second, this elitist view of science places the hard sciences above language, music, philosophy, and other studies that are integral to our human experience. Philosopher Tom Sorell brings greater clarification in that scientism is "a matter of putting too high a value on natural science in comparison with other branches of learning or culture."[2] There are extreme limits to science, not only as it relates to interacting with other disciplines, but also within the hard sciences themselves. The late Nobel Prize Laureate Peter Medawar, himself not a religious man, wrote,

> *"There is no quicker way for a scientist to bring discredit upon himself and upon his profession, than roundly to declare that science knows, or soon will know, the answers to all questions worth asking, and that questions which do not admit a scientific answer are in some way non-questions that simpletons ask and only the gullible profess to be able to answer... The existence of a limit to science is, however, made clear by its inability to answer childlike elementary questions having to do*

with first and last things – questions such as: "How did everything begin?" "What are we all here for?" "What is the point of living."[3]

Of course, theology and philosophy are very useful in pursuing such endeavors, but many modern scientists have not only taken an extreme view of science as the only way to truth but have also devalued other disciplines as not even relevant in modern philosophical inquiry. A chief example of this is the late Stephen Hawking, one of the most brilliant scientists of the twentieth century who, while speaking at a *Google* conference, said, "… almost all of us sometimes wonder: Why are we here? Where do we come from? Traditionally, these questions are for philosophy, but philosophy is dead…. Scientists have become the torchbearers of the discovery in our quest for knowledge."[4]

Hawking's assertion that science is the only avenue of approach to truth and knowledge for questions that the physical sciences were never intended to answer on their own is the epitome of scientism. Scientism, like any other *"ism,"* is an unhealthy view that one specific ideology or opinion is superior to all others not because of truth, but because of the overall belief system. In other words, scientism does not hold to an elite status because science has explained specific laws of nature. Scientism is the result of the absolute claims of science crossing into other disciplines with the same intellectual resolve to truth claims.

It is the foundation for modern chants of "science says," as if there is a universal authority that speaks to all things about truth statements. However, science never says anything, "scientists" do. There is a shared experience of a young college student in England who read a billboard while driving that had a quote from Hawking that we do not need God. The student, a believer in God, reported that he almost drove off of the road and felt a sense of despair as he thought to himself how he could question a great scientist like Stephen Hawking if he said that there was no God.

Scientism is found in our classrooms and is also flourishing in our learning institutions. While it would appear to be a good thing that tenets of scientific theory or methodologies are widely incorporated into classrooms, some researchers within academia related to science education find the phenomena of scientism troubling as it encroaches on other disciplines within academia. Renai Gasparatou from the University of Patras, Greece, shares her concerns with scientism by writing,

> "The idealization of science is partly the reason why we feel we need to impose the so-called scientific terminologies and methodologies to all aspects of our lives, education too. Under this rationale, educational policies today prioritize science, not only in curriculum design but also as a method for educational practice. One might expect that, under the scientistic rationale, science education would thrive. Contrariwise, I will argue that scientism disallows science education to give an accurate image of the sciences. More importantly, I suggest that scientism prevents one of science education's most crucial goals: help students think."[5]

It also appears that scientism has not been the result of a part of scientific theory and its application but more on the psychological effects of modern society's success since the Scientific Revolution.[6] Scientific progress is well noted throughout academia and industry alike and that progress has created an intellectual swagger among other disciplines. However, all that glitters is not gold in the scientific community as there are still serious intellectual gaps in what scientists truly know and understand and what many leading scientists purport to know and understand from the discipline of science.

Even with serious intellectual gaps in both knowledge and

understanding, many leading scientists like Hawking, Dawkins, and Harris, believe(d) that there is no room for God in a scientific world as they mislabel the intellectual pursuits of anyone who believes in God or intelligent design as collectively saying, "God did it, no need to understanding it, let's move on." Such a belief is false and you need only look to the great men who launched the Scientific Revolution to see the dichotomy between God and science is one created by man, not logic.

God vs. Science

The Scientific Revolution was an amazing time in our brief human history. Beginning in the sixteenth-century intellectual giants began to study and develop scientific principles in the world around them. Great scientists, or natural philosophers as they were called, provided intellectual development on a grand scale. Sir Isaac Newton developed a theory to explain the law of gravity, Johannes Kepler's worked on planetary motion, and Robert Boyle, considered to be the first chemist, developed what is now called Boyle's law and also established a systematic approach to scientific inquiry. In addition to great scientific developments, these great men, and many others, shared another common feature and that is they all believed in God as the Creator of everything.

In the *Principia Mathematica*, Isaac Newton wrote,

> *"For by that kind of motion they pass easily through the orbits of the Planets, and with great rapidity; and in their aphelions, where they move the slowest and are detained the longest, they recede to the greatest distances from each other, and thence suffer the least disturbance from their mutual attractions. This most beautiful System of the Sun, Planets, and*

Comets, could only proceed from the counsel and
dominion of an intelligent and powerful Being."[7]

Johannes Kepler made several references to God-centered on
his work, including, but certainly not limited to,

"God is in the numbers."

"I had the intention of becoming a theologian –
but now I see how God is, by my endeavors, also
glorified in astronomy, for the heavens declare the
glory of God.

"The ideas and quantities have been and are in
God from eternity, they are God himself."

Kepler also said, "I much prefer the sharpest
criticism of a single intelligent man to the
thoughtless approval of the masses."[8]

Lastly, Robert Boyle wrote, "God is the author of the universe
and the free establisher of the laws of motion."[9]

These great thinkers who laid the groundwork for scientific
progress made no small matter about their belief in God as the
Creator of the universe and the laws that made up the universe
and apply to the world that we live in. Of course, these men did
not just conclude that God did everything and simply walk away
from science. They knew that God was not a god of chaos, but
the universe was created with order and purpose and therefore
they knew that to study nature was to study, in essence, the works
of God. C.S. Lewis wrote, "Men became scientific because they
expected law in nature, and they expected law in nature because
they believed in a Law-Giver."[10]

The intelligibility of the universe is something that great

scientists took note of in their application of logic. Einstein commented, "The eternal mystery of the world is comprehensible... The fact that it is comprehensible is a miracle."[11] It is absolutely amazing that Newton was able to develop a mathematical formula to describe the law of gravity in his mind. One must ask, "What is the correlation between the human mind and the universe or nature in general?" How do physicists and cosmologists come up with abstract numbers and concepts to describe the universe and its internal laws of operation? That is an amazing accomplishment for a primitive biological brain that is the "product of mindless, unguided processes" and is merely chemicals and matter reacting to external stimuli that evolved from a monkey's mind as Darwin noted in his evolutionary paradox.

Agency vs. Mechanism

In the late nineteenth century, leading up to Darwinian evolution, more scientists began to remove any theological tenets that had been incorporated into the order and design of the universe. What is known in the scientific community as the *Principle of Uniformity* had been ascribed strictly to a product of nature and they removed any scientific inquiry, or the "God-hypothesis." The conclusion was that there is an inherent conflict between God and science. However, Oxford Professor Emeritus, John Lennox, posits a brilliant response to such a drastic approach in scientific methodology when considering the origin and operation of our universe. Lennox used a twentieth-century process to explain why scientists who view a conflict between God and science are taking the wrong approach.

In Lennox's analogy, he asks others to consider the Model-T Ford car. How can we explain the existence of the Model-T? Some would say it is the product of Henry Ford who had the vision and the ability to build the motor car. Others would say the reason we have a motor car is because of the internal combustion engine. Which argument is correct? Well, it depends on the approach you are taking, Henry Ford does not compete with the laws of internal combustion to answer this question. The Model-T is a product of an intelligent being who created it, but there is also the mechanism by which the Model-T came into operation, the existence of the internal combustion engine. Lennox also uses the analogy of boiling water on a stove. It is boiling because molecules are heated to 212° or is it boiling because you want a cup of hot tea?

When Newton discovered a formula for the law of gravity, he did not discard God as the agent of creation but rather marveled at the operational aspect of the universe. Newton did not see God as competing with the laws of physics. Many scientists are seemingly confusing agency and mechanism because they are taking an "either-or" approach position between God and nature or, agency and mechanism as John Lennox often puts it in his arguments. While it is noted elsewhere that atheism is a product of one's worldview rather than one's science, the input of well-known outspoken scientists can certainly shape one's worldview in a manner that appears to be merely scientific.

Unfortunately, many modern scientists such as the late Stephen Hawking, Richard Dawkins, and Sam Harris, just to name a few, have stepped from the scientific world into the world of theology and philosophy to explain to the masses why God does not exist. In his last published book, Stephen Hawking wrote, "There is no need for God in the universe."[12] Scientists have been awarded positions and authority beyond the scope of their selective fields of study. Astronomer Royale and a member of the British Royal Society, Martin Rees, responded to Hawking's assertion that there is no God by saying, "Stephen Hawking knows little about philosophy and even less about theology and we shouldn't ascribe any weight to anything he says on these issues."[13] Nobel Prize Laureate Richard Feynman once said, "Outside of their field, scientists are just as dumb as the rest of us."[13] There is no doubt that many people struggling with faith who read the brilliant, oracular Stephen Hawking's statements that "there is no God or any need for God in our universe," have had their belief or faith shaken to the core by this acclaimed cosmologist.

When Cosmologist Carl Sagan said in his epilogue to the television program *Cosmos*, "The universe is all that there was, all that there is, and all that there ever will be."[14] that should not be taken as the voice of science speaking to us, but a scientist with a personal worldview that God does not exist or that there is no supernatural. There are well-known scientists like Richard Dawkins and the late Stephen Hawking who do not, or did not, believe in the supernatural or God and there are brilliant scientists like Isaac Newton and Robert Boyle, as well as many modern-day successful scientists who believe in God. According to John Lennox, in the twentieth century, 65% of Nobel Prize winners believed in God, and two-thirds of those were "hard scientists."[14]

Descriptive vs. Creative

Modern scientists have over-stepped their discipline in a very problematic way in that they have applied to the physical laws of nature creative abilities that these laws simply do not have. The laws of nature are descriptive, not creative. The laws of mathematics apply to our checking account, but unless we make a deposit, that number will never change. Likewise, when the pool hall closes at night, the cue balls do not roll around because of the laws of motion, the laws of motion apply when an external agent is acting on the ball. When Stephen Hawking wrote, "because there is a law such as gravity, the universe can and will create itself."[15] He was ascribing creative power to the laws of physics. The Judeo-Christian belief is that God created the universe *ex nihilo*, "from nothing." Hawking's statement is saying that a physical law of nature (gravity) created all matter and energy. So, Hawking's "nothing" is not "no thing." The theory of quantum gravity is now being entertained as the antecedent to the singularity that created the Big Bang and thus eliminating an absolute beginning to our universe.

Similarly, Physicist Richard Atkins once said in a debate with John Lennox that "mathematics created the universe."[16] Mathematics is an abstract concept that is generated in the mind of human beings, it would be like a philosopher saying that logic created the universe. Duke University provides a helpful definition in that, Mathematics reveals hidden patterns that help us understand the world around us. "As a science of abstract objects, mathematics relies on logic rather than on observation as its standard of truth, yet employs observation, simulation, and even experimentation as means of discovering truth."[17]

Building on this understanding, Dr. Berj Manoushangian explains,

> *"Math is abstract because numbers are not real entities. They are purely imaginary concepts. We cannot experience numbers. We can make up stories about them, such as "1+1=2", but we can never experience such an operation since there is no such thing as ONE of anything in our experience… When we do math, we are playing a game in a world of imagination."*[18]

When Isaac Newton developed the law of gravity, regarding its operation, he did not attempt to answer the question, "what is gravity?" Newton commented in his works regarding the ontological nature of gravity, *hipotesis non fingo*, which is Latin for "I do not know." Isaac Newton, arguably the greatest scientist in human history said of gravity, "I have no idea what it is" and we are no closer to understanding the ontological make-up of gravity today than in the seventeenth century. Even with the understanding that we do not know what gravity is, Stephen Hawking was willing to step out and ascribe creative power to this unknown force that no one has detailed or precise knowledge of other than its descriptive nature as it relates to gravity within the theory of special relativity.

While remaining on the topic of scientific unknowns, here are a few mysteries that scientists have no definitive answer for: energy, we can measure it ($E=MC^2$), but we have no idea what it is. Light is a mystery to us, even its speed, which can only be measured by the time it takes to go out and reflect back, has to be divided by two, and this measurement is only assumed to calculate the speed of light as a constant. Scientists have no idea what dark matter is or what drives cosmic acceleration (the universe is traveling faster as it gets more spread out). Scientists cannot tell us what the nature of "time" is. Scientists have no idea what consciousness is and, although there have been multiple attempts, scientists have no answer to the question of what it means to be alive.

Ultimately, scientism is the belief that scientists have concrete answers, even when the answers provided are often untested or even unprovable theories, e.g., multiverse theory or the anthropic principle. Scientists have achieved amazing accomplishments over the decades and have made life better for countless people such as discovering the cure for diseases and enhancing our quality of life. The developments of science have turned space travel into the equivalent of an airplane ride and have resolved great challenges to preserve energy and help us live more effective and efficient lives.

Examining the Evidence:

The Scientific Revolution was launched more than three centuries ago by men who believed in the existence of God as a factor in our universe and they did so based largely upon the premise that there was order and design in our universe. As society became more advanced and more modern, the philosophical approach to scientific inquiry excluded God in the form of either a Creator or an intelligent mind behind our universe as the reason for its order and fine-tuning. Intellectuals in the scientific and academic communities have expressed concerns regarding the phenomenon of scientism and its far-reaching effects on learning and the expression of ideas in the classroom. Science and other disciplines should be viewed as unique disciplines that complement, not compete against, one another. The theological question as to "why?" has just as much relevance as to the "how?" to many people and that should never bring discredit upon them, but it does.

Many outspoken atheists have caricatured other scientists using terms such as "creationists" or those who subscribe to Intelligent Design as "*ID*iots." Furthermore, they have made accusations that these intelligent scientists are engaging in pseudo-science for simply asking questions about the extreme fine-tuning of our universe as well as the phenomenon of spontaneous life, which the discipline of science cannot answer. Science remains unable to answer basic questions about our universe and to presume that it does brings discredit upon the profession and practice of scientific inquiry.

"For since the creation of the world His invisible attributes, that is, His eternal power and divine nature, have been clearly perceived, being understood by what has been made, so that they are without excuse."

Romans 1:20

6 Modus Operandi

Modus Operandi in Latin translates into English as "method of operation" or "M.O." When law enforcement looks at evidence from a series of connected crimes, they look for a specific method of operation to pinpoint an offender when caught. Sex offenders often have unique mannerisms, something that they say or do when carrying out a violent attack on a victim. Burglars have an M.O. that they use whenever trying to ensure a resident is not home. A common M.O. involves knocking on the front door with a ruse about needing to call someone in case the homeowner answers the door and, when they do not, they force entry into the home. The list goes on and on, but it is the M.O. that enables law enforcement to quickly identify unique traits linked with specific suspects and potentially clear cases with an arrest even when a suspect does not admit or confess to those specific crimes.

When I began my investigation into the worldview and arguments by outspoken, "leading," atheists, I was not only bringing my theological background but my investigative skills in fact-finding and evidentiary analysis. I had served over twenty years in law enforcement as a detective and police supervisor with countless visits to courtrooms for hearings and trials. I had developed complex cases involving felony investigations requiring interview and interrogation plans, worked with experts from the FBI office regarding computer forensic exams, and had used DNA collection and hand-writing analysis to build criminal cases based on facts.

I was now serving as an Inspector General for the Department of the Army – trained and required to be an impartial fact-finder involving allegations and complaints that could potentially derail someone's career. Serving as an impartial fact-finder is challenging at times whenever individuals are filing a complaint about something that has had an impact on their career or their personal life. However, in many cases, the hardship is not the result of something that someone has done but is often the result of the actual complainant failing to do something like complete a requirement for promotion or pay. Going into complaints or allegations as a neutral fact-finder prevents an Inspector General from making mistakes or false inferences. I was now warming up to take on what I perceived to be an intellectual crucible that would involve analyzing complex arguments from leading atheists and scientists against the existence of God from an evidentiary standpoint and remaining neutral on the facts of the argument.

It is important to note the "evidentiary" aspect of my research. I believe in God, and I was not looking to overturn that belief, but I wanted to take on leading arguments by intelligent men and women who were making significant claims against the existence of a god, specifically, the God of the Bible. I was prepared to examine the evidence presented by leading atheists and hope that I could address that evidence through fair, impartial fact-finding. Whatever scientific or historical claim they would present against the existence of God would be put against everything that I learned or would learn about my faith and my worldview.

What I found after watching hours and hours of debates, listening to extensive interviews, reading books, and conducting vast amounts of peer-viewed research on Darwinian evolution was that there are several inherent problems within the theory and atheism in general. These were not problems that I discovered *per se* but were issues and questions raised by both proponents and opponents of Darwinian evolution. Of course, the outspoken atheists, or "new-atheists" as the term now applies, were not among proponents of evolution questioning any aspect of the theory. Their responses were always attacking other worldviews or arguments for God or intelligent design and belittling intelligent, respectful scientists in their field.

A reasonable analysis of the approach that Darwinian evolutionists take to argue their point is universal and has seemingly evolved into a boilerplate approach from leading evolutionists. Their arguments for evolution are bolstered by their systematic attacks on the validity of any approach or evidence involving God or intelligent design behind creation. Moreover, their arguments and attacks against "creationists" are structured and, for the most part, unchanging in the specific approach or M.O., which largely involves redefining terms and arguments made by those who believe in a supernatural or outside cause to our universe as well as life on earth.

God-of-the-Gaps

When conducting research in any field, first and foremost you must define terms and variables that you are researching or measuring. Atheists like Richard Dawkins, Sam Harris, and other "new atheists" automatically label anyone who does not subscribe to Darwinian evolution as "creationists." The approach that these individuals take to address the theory of intelligent design or theism is simply to attack the intellectual level of the person and also the character of God as described in Bible. In his book, *The God Delusion* Dawkins writes,

"The God of the Old Testament is arguably the most unpleasant character in all fiction: jealous and proud of it; a petty, unjust, unforgiving control-freak; a vindictive, bloodthirsty ethnic cleanser; a misogynistic, homophobic, racist, infanticidal, genocidal, filicidal, pestilential, megalomaniacal, sadomasochistic, capriciously malevolent bully."

"Creationists eagerly seek a gap in present-day knowledge or

understanding. If an apparent gap is found, it is assumed that God, by default, must fill it."[1]

Sam Harris follows a similar vein in his book, *The End of Faith,*

"A close study of our holy books reveals that the God of Abraham is a ridiculous fellow—capricious, petulant, and cruel—and one with whom a covenant is little guarantee of health or happiness. If these are the characteristics of God, then the worst among us have been created far more in his image than we ever could have hoped."

"The idea that any one of our religions represents the infallible word of the One True God requires an encyclopedic ignorance of history, mythology, and art even to be entertained—as the beliefs, rituals, and iconography of each of our religions attest to centuries of cross-pollination among them."[2]

Of course, the Late Christopher Hitchens was not to be outdone in an attack of (Christian) theists by saying, "For God so loved the world, that he gave his only begotten Son, that whosoever believeth in him will believeth in anything. - Hitchens 3:16."[3] Again, Hitchens is attacking the intellectual level of people who believe in God and not the argument itself in this instance. Hitchens, however, was willing to acknowledge the substantive argument of intelligent design when he attested, "I think every one of us picks the 'fine-tuning' one as the most intriguing" of the arguments for intelligent design." He also says, "You have to spend time thinking about it, working on it. It's not trivial. We all say that."[4]

The approach that these atheists often make, or made in Hitchens' case, is called an *ad hominem* approach to an argument. It is Latin for "to the person" and it involves attacking an individual presenting an argument as opposed to challenging the evidence presented by an individual. When I served as a detective working with victims of assault, I would sometimes inform the victim I was working with that when the evidence is overwhelming against a defendant, the defense attorney often has no other course of action in a trial but to attack the victim's character. The purpose of such an attack is to get the victim upset or to appear irrational or untrustworthy to the jury or judge to overshadow significant evidence leading to an unfavorable verdict or outcome for the defendant.

Whether intentional or not, atheists typically like to present emotionally charged pictures of God, religion, or anything that challenges their worldview to attack God's character or the intellect of someone who believes in God. This type of attack also includes people who simply argue for intelligent design. Aggressive atheists often attempt to stupefy people with religious rhetoric and then, like the quintessential shell-game at the state fair, switch commentary about the God of creation or the Bible with mythic, primordial gods by placing him in the category of *Zeus* or *Poseidon*. In an instant, an atheist may have someone debating the existence of God while they are referring to Greek gods of mythology as if there is an attempt to defend a god of lightning or thunder or some other created entity that serves in the place of unexplained phenomena that science has yet to resolve.

In a debate with Frank Turek, atheist Dave Silverman surprisingly opened up his argument against the belief in God with a screen that read, "God of the Gaps" = "I don't know = Proof of a god, which is no proof at all.[4] Silverman served as the Vice President of American Atheists, and his leadoff argument against theism was the "god-of-the-gaps" argument. This approach was shockingly elementary and lacking in any qualified substance. The phenomena of created gods are nowhere in the literature for theists or intelligent design proponents. Such confusing rhetoric serves as an instrument to logically elevate science above a false view of faith in that created gods are at the center of theism or serves as the logical basis in arguments for intelligent design. Greek mythology has these created gods as the substance of the universe, not outside of the universe, and certainly not the one true God who created the universe.

Faith and our Fathers

Paralleling Darwin's work in the physical world was the work of Sigmund Freud in the psychoanalytic world. Darwinian evolution strongly influenced Freud and the result was the groundbreaking theories of Freud in evolutionary and hereditary causes of mental illness.[5] Freud believed that religious people exhibited the same traits as individuals suffering from neurotic conditions who displayed commitments to rituals and suffered from neurosis when those rituals were violated.[6] Freud not only believed that the neurotic conditions were passed from the parents, but he also believed that religious people, specifically males, experienced conflict with their father as well as an innate drive for hegemonic power.[7] Freud, himself a staunch atheist, laid the groundwork for modern-day atheists to theorize the irrational role that religion plays in society. The late Christopher Hitchens was among the "new atheists" to weave Freudian thought into his arguments against religion by concluding that religious people were "weak-minded and childish."[8] Not to be outdone, fellow atheists Richard Dawkins and Sam Harris frequently refer to religious people as having psychological maladies.

Interestingly, on the topics of faith, fathers, and psychological distress, many renowned atheists including Nietzsche, Bertrand Russell, and Sartre all lost their fathers at a very young age.[9] Other atheists like Freud, Marx, and Feuerbach had fathers whom they despised because of their conduct, Freud complained to a colleague that his father was a sexual pervert.[10] Perhaps the question should be pondered if that acknowledgment played some role in Freud's obsession with sex as the prime motivator for human subconscious thought and behavior. While there are at least three predominant theories as reasons why someone subscribes to atheism, the one reason that most likely fits into the theory of an abusive father or some authority figure is frustration theory.[11] This analysis only draws a unique distinction of leading atheists within the context of claims that religious people use their faith as a crutch or support system.

Richard Dawkins takes the pangs of religion and its abuses on children by authority figures to partially validate his disdain for religion. One example he gives is the story of Edgardo Mortara, a nineteenth-century Italian boy who was forcibly taken from his Jewish parents by the Catholic Church. Of course, Dawkins makes the broad leap that such actions are commonplace today and of course, that the priests who stole this child were morally wrong and not just "dancing to their DNA." Dawkins goes on to speak of this behavior that, "has nothing to do with sense, and everything to do with religion"[12] and ties this horrific behavior to religious practices today as commonplace. Dawkins' story is filled with emotional rhetoric complete with italicized adjectives and exclamation points as if the readers cannot comprehend for themselves the seriousness of these wrongs. However, the glaring inconsistency of Dawkins' naturalistic worldview, where the universe is nothing but "blind, pitiless indifference," and his moral contempt for any religious system, violates the basic tenets of logic because, again, we are just biological entities dancing to our DNA.

While Dawkins is most likely an exceptional biologists and zoologist, he reaches into other academic disciplines such as psychology, sociology, philosophy, and theology and demands the same academic veracity from his followers. As it has been noted previously, statements by scientists are not necessarily statements of science. Scientists do not get to transfer their authority in science to different academic disciplines. However, in "The God Delusion," Richard Dawkins cites only one psychiatric journal as a source document in over four hundred pages arguing against belief in God in a book that includes a psychiatric disorder in its title.[13] Apparently more than three million inquiring minds thought this was not an issue to be considered.

Dawkins believes that faith is something that is passed down to our children, which is true in many cases. Dawkins also concludes that faith can be "very, very dangerous, and to deliberately plant it into a vulnerable mind of an innocent child is a grievous wrong."[14] The late Christopher Hitchens echoes Dawkins' sentiment by concluding, "if religious instruction were not allowed until the child had attained the age of reason, we would be living in quite a different world."[15] Hitchens and other outspoken atheists have proclaimed that the illogical or irrational beliefs of a deity or belief in an afterlife are the product of undue influence and intellectual naivety of genealogy or heritage.

Richard Dawkins has argued that he will debate priests, rabbis, and preachers on the detrimental effect of religion on society and people in general. It is unfortunate that in the process of his lecture circuits and debates he has never been paired up with psychiatrists or psychologists about the maladies of religion or belief in God. Dawkins, and many other outspoken atheists, speak of the ills of religion and spirituality on people as if it were drug abuse or alcoholism to which no one benefits. However, in an example of "scientism," Dawkins and other outspoken atheists who attack religion and aspects of faith demonstrate no awareness of how scientists and physicians in the field of psychology have developed voluminous research regarding the positive effects of religion and faith on individuals.

Dr. Rob Whitley has "amassed research that indicates higher levels of religious belief and practice is associated with better mental health."[16] The work that Whitley speaks of as being "amassed" comes from peer-reviewed research in the field of psychiatry. Research at the acclaimed Mayo Clinic has included collected data that reveals religiously involved persons lived longer.[17] Further studies have shown that spirituality has a positive impact on depression, anxiety and there is an inverse relationship between spirituality and suicidal ideation.[18] An inverse relationship simply means that when one variable goes up, the other goes down, and vice versa. It would also mean that spirituality can moderate the phenomenon of suicide ideation in that introducing spirituality would, in theory, lowers suicidal ideation in people.

It is quite apparent that had Dawkins wanted to use peer-reviewed data as a resource for his books or speaking engagements on the ills of religion or spirituality, he need not have to search for long. However, emotion and rhetoric serve him better than the facts attained from the field of psychology. Richard Dawkins was quoted as recently saying, "What I say in biology has become pretty much orthodoxy,"[19] but when reviewing the published scientific papers within his field the findings are surprisingly scant for this former Oxford Professor at fewer than twenty-five peer-reviewed articles in his first three decades in academia.[20]

Examining the Evidence: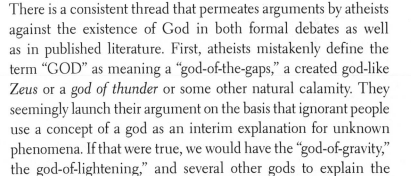

There is a consistent thread that permeates arguments by atheists against the existence of God in both formal debates as well as in published literature. First, atheists mistakenly define the term "GOD" as meaning a "god-of-the-gaps," a created god-like *Zeus* or a *god of thunder* or some other natural calamity. They seemingly launch their argument on the basis that ignorant people use a concept of a god as an interim explanation for unknown phenomena. If that were true, we would have the "god-of-gravity," the god-of-lightening," and several other gods to explain the fundamental forces in our universe because, although we have laws that describe these forces, we do not know ontologically what they are and probably never will.

It also becomes clear that atheists not only attack the character and nature of God, as believed in theism, but they attack or challenge the intellectual character of theists who believe that

God or an intelligent mind could be behind spontaneous creation and complex life that operates on a computer-like code. Calling people idiots, insane, or some other unpleasantry violates the civilized process that is supposed to be facilitated in a debate. Moreover, atheists often argue that a person normally would not become a theist or religious if left to their natural tendencies, but rather, parents, culture, or religion itself imposes upon the intellect of the young and impressionable the concept of a god. Of course, atheists steer clear of the historical tendency for leading atheists to have come from a home either where a father was absent either literally or figuratively. The research speaks to the psychological trauma of growing up in a family without a father (see Ch. 10, *Evil and Suffering*).

The M.O. of atheists is not to investigate claims of the potential of God or intelligence, but to reject the idea from its initial consideration. They defend their a priori belief that there is no God by going on the offensive and attacking the validity of Scripture or the intellectual prowess of scientists who do not believe as they do on this important issue. The most important question in life as it related to who we are and who God is should be met with full consideration and not downplayed because we do not want there to be a god or we do not like the person(s) arguing for the existence of God.

"The heart of the righteous ponders how to answer...."

7   Not a Chance!

The intellectual stance of atheists is that nature is responsible for creating all matter, energy, and life. Due to their argument against a Creator or intelligence behind complex life and the fine-tuning of the universe, the only option for a naturalist or materialist is to create their own "god-of-the-gaps," namely *chance*. Evolutionists acknowledge, "Within biology, a clear understanding of probability concepts such as chance and randomness is necessary for understanding evolutionary processes.[1] However, evolutionists go on to describe chance, not in probability terms, but in being tied directly to the evolutionary force of natural selection. In an attempt to provide a clear definition of "chance," Louis Mead and Eugenie Scott, acknowledge the confusion in this evolutionary term but spend most of their effort defining what chance is not rather than providing a cogent explanation of the Darwinian application of chance.

> *"Although creationists discuss the "improbability" of an amino acid sequence assembling by "chance," they use "by chance" primarily to mean "with no planning or purpose." The nonscientific public, encouraged by antievolutionists, contrasts "natural" with "designed," not realizing that a natural process such as natural selection can produce design, in the sense of complex, functioning structures."[2]*

The role of chance, in the views of leading advocates for Darwinian evolution, appears to ascribe a creative function to "chance." Chance is not throwing dice to see if they end up on double-sixes. Chance, via natural selection, moves the dice and randomness comes into play. However, evolution is still viewed as "a game of chance."[3] Still, there remains significant ambiguity in defining "chance" in efforts to synthesize the content in peer-reviewed journals and scientific periodicals in hopes of obtaining a clearly defined term that works in concert with randomness and natural selection. Perhaps the fanfare from hardcore evolutionists that teachers are not teaching evolution, or at least is serving as a source of misconception for students about evolution[4], should be evaluated within the context of a teacher's understanding of the complex and ambiguous terms that even dedicates evolutionists struggle to define.

While a concrete definition of chance is not solid, developments in science and technology have enabled us to consider the focus of evolutionary studies. The result of the advances in technology has created greater problems for evolutionary theory than ambiguous terms that only the most advanced in the field of biology express confidence in understanding. Almost 100 years after *Origin* was published, the double-helix was discovered and eventually gave way to the amazing complexity of human DNA. Just as Darwin could have never imagined the complexity of a human cell when he theorized that all life evolved from a single globular cell, scientists could hardly imagine the complexity of information contained in the double-helix that serves as a complex code for cell development.

In the Beginning, Well, Almost

It is important to understand that when speaking of evolution, evolution does not typically include the origins of life in research.

Remember back in chapter three, it was as if the theory of evolution starts with "Chapter 2" in the collective explanation of life. However, Darwinian evolutionists do assume that life did start through random mutations as non-living chemicals developed into life in what is referred to as abiogenesis. Three different branches of science work with abiogenesis theory: geophysical, chemical, and biological.[4] At the heart of the matter are of course the chemical processes that are needed to coalesce within a specific geophysical environment to eventually form biological life.

The logical response to Darwinian evolutions must begin with an understanding of the chemicals that existed in the way that evolutionists argue that life emerged, and the chance of those chemicals coming together to form a complex cell that was later able to mutate into higher forms necessary to start and sustain life. Dr. Dean Kenyon, a foremost scientist who helped launched the intelligent design movement said, *"It is an enormous problem, how you could get together in one tiny, sub-microscopic volume of the primitive ocean all of the hundreds of different molecular components you would need for a self-replicating cycle to be established."*[5] To bolster Dr. Kenyon's analysis involving probability, Stephen Meyer weighs heavily on the works of William Dembski as a starting point for further evidentiary analysis on the probability of spontaneous life forming and thriving in conditions that evolutionists themselves have determined to have been present when the earth and estimated 4.5 billion years ago, approximately 9 billion years after the *Big Bang*, which is a significant timeline for Meyer's analysis.

The dice of chance in this game of probability are amino acids that form proteins. The parameters for the game of probability that life started spontaneously from non-living matter as a result of chemicals were established by Dembski as the numbers of seconds since the Big Bang, roughly 10^{16} seconds.[6] Meyer's analysis reveals that "the probability of a sufficient number of amino acids to align to create even a minimally complex cell by chance is $10^{41,000}$"[7]

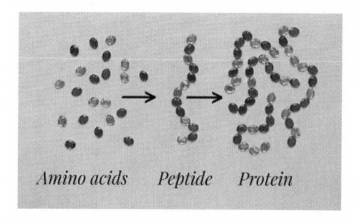

Amino acids   Peptide   Protein

Evolutionists argue that both time and chance serve an adequate response to any complex issue. The improbable can be set aside in the name of evolution and chance because the age of the universe vastly outweighs any arguments against improbability. As such, atheists may conclude that twenty amino acids can align in a specific order and sequence through time and by chance to form enough proteins necessary to start life. Looking at protein sequencing requirements we are informed that, "Proteins coded in the human genome are expected to number about 3.5×10^4. If any combinations of 20 amino acids are equally possible, there are 1.3×10^{130} possible amino acid sequences in proteins."[8] Numbers such as these exceed reasonableness when combined with only time and chance, but also, this does not even address the first cells believed by naturalists to have emerged spontaneously from non-living matter.

In 1953 the Miller-Urey experiment created promise and fanfare after a few amino acids surfaced in a glass tube or flask in a laboratory setting. The chemical product of the experiment was not even close to being enough to build a protein, remember you need twenty amino acids in perfect sequence. Furthermore, research reveals that the chemical environment that was used in this early experiment included gases that were not neutral to building amino acids. Earlier, reference was made to the three fields that are required for investigation in abiogenesis theory: geophysical, chemical, and biological.

Not only does the probability of random amino acids forming a functional protein appear impossible, but there is also another problem for the Miller-Urey experiment. The gases used in the experiment, namely methane and ammonia did not exist in large amounts on early planet earth.[9] A follow-up experiment was conducted thirty years later with the *correct* gases and it was "discovered that the reactions were producing chemicals (nitrites) which destroy amino acids as quickly as they form."[10] This does not bode well for anyone arguing that scientists were able to create the building blocks of the human cell in an experiment.

Unfortunately, when you look up the Miller-Urey experiment on "KhanAcademy.org," a website described as a "personalized learning experience resource for all ages," you find this failed experiment is described as "the first evidence that organic molecules needed for life could be formed from inorganic chemicals."[11] Similarly, the *Smithsonian Magazine* references the Miller-Urey experiment as a success in that "Miller had created a broth of amino acids."[12] Again, science is not the problem, there is nothing wrong with doing an experiment correctly and recording the results. However, promoting a failed experiment as an explanation for the origin of life from non-organic chemicals is very problematic. The only two options for promoting such a failed experiment as a landmark success are that there is a lack of knowledge in how the experiment was conducted or that the results of the experiment were simply ignored – and neither of the two is a good option for scientific advancement.

The Code of Life

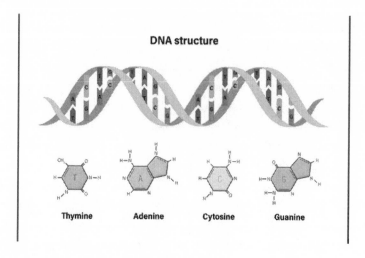

DNA structure

Thymine   Adenine   Cytosine   Guanine

The amino acids that form into proteins do so through a four-character code located along the baseline of the double-helix. The letters A – T – C – G serve as the alphabetic code that informs the different types of proteins. They are the four nitrogen bases that serve as base pairs that create information for proteins and cellular machinery to operate through transcription. Once the genetic coding process adds the twentieth and final amino acid in the chain the protein breaks off and forms the specific shape and function that was communicated to it. Ultimately, the genetic code in our body is 3.4 billion letters long, all in perfect sequence, to communicate instructional code for life.

In his book, *Signature in the Cell,* Dr. Stephen Meyer discusses his research into the bonding process of nucleotide bases. What has been discovered through bio-chemistry is that the chemistry in the nucleotide patterns in the DNA are "equivalent." In other words, the bonding of the code that makes up the messaging code is not determined by chemicals. Meyer notes, "There are no significant forces of attraction between the individual letters that determine their arrangements."[13] This implies that there is a force outside of chemistry or biology that directs the alignment of the twenty amino acids that ultimately form every protein within a cell. Whatever is making A-T-C-G align in a specific sequence to form protein molecules cannot be examined under a microscope!

Meyer, who is also an educator, uses a very basic visual aid to demonstrate this process in lectures, an elementary child's magnetic whiteboard where any letter can stick to the board in any arrangement because of an identical magnetic attraction among the different letters. The same process is true regarding the chemical composition where Meyer notes, "there are no differential forces of attraction between the DNA bases and the sites on the sugar-phosphate backbone [of the double-helix]"[14]. However, for proponents of Darwinian evolution, i.e., time and chance solve all problems, there not only exists the highly complex problem of DNA coding within the body in an inexplicable manner but also creating new information to create new and distinct proteins for new species.[15]

Bill Gates, who is assumingly aware of the DNA code, has been quoted as saying, "DNA is like a computer program but far, far more advanced than any software ever created."[16] Gates' commentary on the amazing information in the DNA code is spot-on, but perhaps Gates himself failed to acknowledge the depths of his acknowledgment. Our DNA code, with 3.4 billion digits of code perfectly aligned, does have a programmer because you do not get information without a mind. Scientists who hold to intelligent design argue that letters, digital information, or any form of code cannot be a product of mere time + matter + chance, especially when there is no identifiable biochemical driver to align the code itself.

Assume that you are in a jet aircraft flying over the ocean and you looked down and observed the letters H E L P spelled out in large logs on the beach of a seemingly deserted island in the middle of the ocean. Would you inform the flight crew of what you observed so they could plot the coordinates for a response?

Why not simply reflect to yourself how long it must have taken for the forces of nature to align downed trees in such a unique pattern as to only appear to write "help"? Why do the words "HELP" communicate something to you? Information is more than an absolute reduction to physics and chemistry just as these words you are reading now convey more than ink on paper.

Richard Dawkins himself acknowledges the complexity of the information but concludes, based on evolution alone, that it is only "the appearance of design." It reminds me of the slap-comedy "Police Squad" with Detective Frank Drebin trying to move people along after a fiery car crashes into a fireworks factory. There are massive, beautiful explosions going off in the sky above the building and Detective Drebin is shouting to the gathering crowd, "Let's move along people… nothing to see here!"

There is a massive complex code that exceeds any computer code ever written that does not align according to a preset chemical requirement to communicate data to build protein molecules and we expect a simple answer of, "well, it's just chance and evolution." It must be noted that a summary of evidence into this amazing phenomenon has only been briefly introduced in this section. The amazing complexity of what is going on in human DNA has been more thoroughly discussed in books such as *Signature in the Cell* and *Darwin's Black Box: The Biochemical Challenges to Evolution*. Furthermore, the work of leading organic chemist Dr. James Tour, who has more than 700 peer-reviewed publications, can be viewed on *YouTube* as well as in more scholarly research to highlight the problems of evolution as it related to biochemistry.

Irreducible Complexity

Michael Behe, professor, and biochemist at Lehigh University was first to coin the term "irreducible complexity, which he defined as *"a single system which is necessarily composed of several well-matched, interacting parts that contribute to the basic function, and where the removal of any one of the parts causes the system to effectively cease functioning.*"[17] The cell has been compared to a highly efficient factory that collects, stores, and distributes "products" within several different departments within the cell factory. Within the cell, complex proteins are formed through precise information that enables living organisms to build and sustain life. Understandably, Darwin and his contemporaries did not possess a true understanding of the grand complexity of the cell. One of the leading contemporaries among Darwin's colleagues was G.H. Lewes who wrote,

> *"Not let our glance pass on to the Cell. Here we have the first recognized differentiation of structure, in the appearance of a nucleus amid the protoplasm. The nucleus is chemically different from the substance which surrounds it; and although perhaps exaggerated importance has been attributed to this nucleus, and mysterious powers have been ascribed to it, yet as an essential constituent of the cell commands attention. Indeed, according to most investigations, the definition of a cell is a "nucleus with surrounding protoplasm."*[18]

Behe's research has been among the first to propose the question," is it reasonable to ask if the theory of evolution still seems to be a good explanation of life?"[19] One primary reason for this argument is Darwin himself who wrote in *Origin*, "If it could be demonstrated that any complex organ existed, which could not possibly have been formed by numerous, successive, slight modifications, my theory would absolutely break down. But I can find no such case."[20] Darwin not only failed to appreciate even the fundamental operation of a cell, but he could have never known about the molecular machines that operate inside the cell.

The molecular protein machines operating within the human

cell are beyond human comprehension. Arguably the most sophisticated of the molecular machines operating in our body is the bacterial flagellar motor that operates at a level far beyond human technology or understanding. The bacterial flagellar motor (BFM) is described by Behe as an outboard motor that bacteria use to swim with its long filamentous tail that acts as a propeller. The propeller is attached to the drive shaft through the hook region, which acts as a universal joint, the drive shaft is attached to the motor, which uses a flow of acid or sodium ion from outside of the cell to the inside of the cell to power rotation. The BFM can rotate at speeds of over 100,000 RPMs, stop on a quarter turn, and reverse direction.[21] To provide a reference to the amazing engineering feats the BFM achieves, most jet engines rotate at a maximum of 15,000 RPMs.

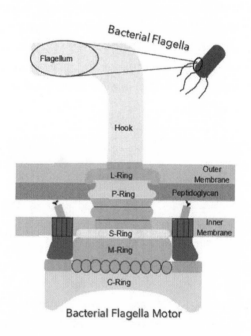

Bacterial Flagella Motor

It can be safe to assume that if the BFM is operating at 100,000 RPMs, and can stop and change rotational direction virtually instantaneously, there would be a serious problem if all of the components were not operating at maximum efficiency or yet, were missing altogether because the part had not evolved. It is the complex code previously described that provides the detailed engineering instructions to make the molecular machine we call BFM. To take away that code or any part of the BFM as a less evolved motor can be argued in a hypothesis by Darwinian evolutionists, but in all actuality, common sense and logic should rule the day.

There are certainly more examples of the problems that irreducible complexity poses for Darwinian evolutionists. The blood clotting cascade in the body as well as the eye, which Darwin himself acknowledged,

> *"To suppose that the eye with all its inimitable contrivances for adjusting the focus to different distances, for admitting different amounts of light, and for the correction of spherical and chromatic aberration, could have been formed by natural selection, seems, I freely confess, absurd in the highest degree."*[22]

However, Darwinian evolutionists have engaged in intellectual acrobatics to respond to these challenges. Some evolutionists say the quote by Darwin is taken way out of context and others view it more directly when followed by the conclusion that they have discovered how the eye likely evolved.

A deeper analysis of the problem will find prominent scientists acknowledging there is no answer for such complexity in a Darwinian worldview. The non-profit website, *Dissent From Darwin*, captures a host of professionals in their field who present intellectual challenges to the panaceas that have been proclaimed in Darwinian evolution. One specific conclusion by Biochemist Franklin Harold is that "There are presently no detailed Darwinian accounts of the evolution of any biochemical or cellular system, only a variety of wishful speculations."[23]

Looking to the Stars

The late Christopher Hitchens, although himself not a scientists, once commented that microscopes and telescopes have made religion obsolete in answering questions of any importance. Quite the contrary, the microscope has resulted in discoveries that should drastically shake the confidence of an atheist or anyone who subscribes to Darwinian evolution. As for the telescope, it has been instrumental in what has been described as a marriage made in the heavens between observational and theoretical astronomy. Chief among the discoveries has been what has been coined as the "goldilocks enigma," taken from the childhood story of *Goldilocks and the Three Bears.*

The Goldilocks enigma or "mystery," refers to the amazing fine-tuning of our universe and the laws of physics that are present and required to host carbon-based life. Again, defining terms is critical when considering variables within positions, theories, or arguments. The conjunctive word *"fine-tuning"* is referring to the exquisite fine-tuning of our universe with the ability to host carbon-based life because of the finely-tuned parameters that exist in our universe and for our planet. Scientists and philosophers can posit three alternatives to choose from to explain the existence of a finely-tuned universe:

- First, our universe is the way it is simply by chance.
- Second, our universe is one of many universes, but this just happens to be the one suitable for life (still based on chance).
- Third, our universe has a Designer who created our universe and our planet suitable to host carbon-based life.

Putting these three alternatives on equal intellectual levels will help examine the evidence that scientific discoveries have provided. Conclusions from the evidence presented must lead to one of the three aforementioned alternatives. To help arrive at any one of the alternatives, the evidence examined should lead someone to what has been called an "inference to the best explanation." Such an approach should mitigate the effect of personal bias or at least reveal more clearly when personal bias is affecting potential conclusions. Of course, this process cannot fully play out if one of the alternatives is removed from the list of potential causes and that can only be done through a worldview, not science. The scientific process does not rule out a Designer, science is a process to examine evidence, and it is argued here, that the high improbability of the first two "best explanations" necessarily leads to the third option which points to a Designer or Creator for our universe.

It does appear that there is a desperate attempt to avoid the necessary conclusions of fine-tuning, which some atheists postulate as the strongest evidence for a Designer. Science journalist Tim Folger sums up this position well for *Discover Magazine*, "Our universe is perfectly tailored for life. That may be the work of God or the result of our universe being one of many... Call it a fluke, a mystery, a miracle. Or call it the biggest problem in physics. Short of invoking a benevolent creator, many physicists see only one possible explanation: Our universe may be but one of perhaps infinitely many universes in an inconceivably vast multiverse."[24]

Individuals within the scientific community acknowledge the problematic evidence of a Designer in the overall analysis. Consider the lengthy explanation of fine-tuning from Ella Anderson's commentary on the validity of the Multiverse theory as part of an unseen solution to the need for a Designer,

The strength of the electromagnetic force is .0073. The mass of the electron, as a fraction of the proton's mass, is .00054. The formation of heavier elements depends on a number called Epsilon (measuring the amount of hydrogen that converts into helium), a figure equal to .007. The strength of the electric force is N: 10^{36} and stands as a show of gravity's weakness in our dimension. Numbers *like these describe the particles of our world and the forces which guide their motion and bind them together. But there is one number, in particular, sometimes known as lambda, that has caused many scientists to believe the universe is precise. So finely-tuned that it's unlikely to be accidental. Instead, it seems almost designed...* Why, as we uncover more and more of the delicate numbers behind our laws of physics (and thus our existence), does it feel like the universe was tailor-made for life?" [25]

Anderson presents a very cogent argument for design but saves the day with the final analysis that the Multiverse theory would stipulate that we are no longer a product of unique design, but rather of statistical probability. She argues for the embracing of an unprovable theory as a solution to our amazing design by arguing, "To have an accurate understanding of the universe we must take into account what we can't see just as much as what we can. There exist all around us invisible worlds, after all."[26] This is a very disappointing conclusion and is not an "inference to the best explanation" as to the fine-tuning of our universe.

The argument has been displayed here that for the cosmologists, it is permissible to take in the potential of an unseen world (or universe), but to consider, an unseen Designer launches us beyond the realms of reason or science and therefore it must be necessarily excluded from theories of causality. There is widespread agreement that our universe is not the product of blind-chance based on all of the known factors presented. There are some revealing conclusions from scientists from all camps on the complexity of our universe that requires more than a mere chance for our universe and planet to host carbon-based life.

However, although Einstein and Hawking both concluded that the universe had a beginning, the complex fine-tuning of the universe is driving some cosmologists away from such conclusions to adopt a theory of an infinite number of universes. Following the death of a universe, a new and subsequent one is born through cosmic inflation and microscopic fluctuations that form into matter in what is believed to be a quantum field. Quantum fluctuations in cosmology create a hopeful sense among materialists that the universe never had a beginning to ease the philosophical tension that comes with a universe that has a beginning as well as apparent design.

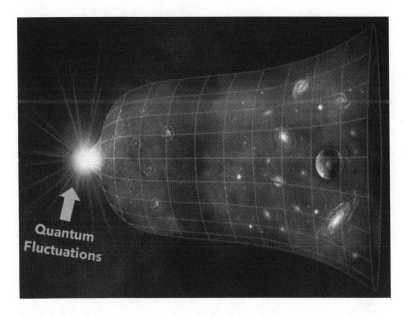

Before Hawking's death, he worked with Thomas Hertog to "scale down" the multiverse theory. Hawking had stated previously in an interview, "I have never been a fan of the multiverse."[27] It appears highly questionable that cosmologists are ready to walk away from a universe that had a beginning and once again rest on the belief that the universe always existed albeit through cosmic fluctuations. The colloquial saying, "Whatever helps you sleep at night" seems appropriate to this approach to cosmological theory considering its broad leap of faith.

Examining the Evidence: 🔍

There is a saying common in law enforcement, "Criminals have to get lucky every time they commit a crime, but police only have to be lucky once to catch them." I have responded to some luck in such cases… a discarded cigarette from a burglary that contains someone's DNA, a jailhouse recording where a defendant asks his mom to be an alibi for him after explaining in detail what and where he did what he did, a criminal dropping his ID or cell phone at the scene of a robbery.

Are we the product of just dumb luck out of all the highly improbable numbers for life and our existence? Our DNA code of 3.4 billion letters is in perfect sequence. Mathematician John Lennox shares that a "ten-word sentence" can be arranged in 3,628,800 different ways![28, 29] How might things go array if we had to randomly arrange 4 letters, $A - G - C - T$ that represent the chemical code of our DNA in a perfect sequence so long that it would take you more than thirty years (reading 24 hours each day) to read the code if it were placed on paper?

As for the complexity in the stars, just a small argument has been presented in this chapter, with no references for the highly improbable factors that must be present for our planet alone to host life. A great educational video on *YouTube* is "The Privileged Planet," if you are more into reading, a book by the same title was published by Guillermo Gonzales, *et al.*, that will provide amazing details about our planet. Even our location in the *Milky Way* is perfectly positioned to see deep out into space. In the 1970s when the Voyager was turned around to photograph our sun and planetary system a breath-taking distinction was captured in a photograph. Commentary by Carl Sagan, of all people, included "Because of the reflection of sunlight the Earth seems to be sitting in a beam of light as if there were some special significance to this small world… (Sagan later wrote that it was just an "accident" of where it is located).[30] The improbability and chance that our universe was created out of nothing and perfectly aligned to create a planet that had to have too many features to assign to chance for life to exist.

"By faith we understand that the world has been created by the word of God so that what is seen has not been made out of things that are visible."

Hebrews 11:3

8   Has God Really Said?

It has already been referenced that natural revelation, as it is called, is a way that God communicates with his creation. As referenced earlier, great scientists necessitated or concluded a lawgiver because they knew that the laws of nature were not chaotic, but orderly and predictive. We can trust the physical laws of nature, but what about God's other revelation? Has the God who created the endless expanse of a finely-tuned universe and the complexity of human DNA communicated specifically to us? If so, how can we be sure that God has revealed Himself in a special way through his word and the Bible is not just the voice of well-meaning men who call themselves a prophet or were designated to lead in some capacity? What is so special about "special revelation" and what can it tell us?

Special revelation is God speaking directly to his creation. To achieve this communication, God-inspired ordinary men to speak and write while being inspired by the Holy Spirit as they put pen to parchment. The Bible even communicates to us that it is inspired, 2 Timothy 3:16, *All Scripture is inspired by God and is beneficial for teaching, for rebuke, for correction, for training in righteousness.* But that's quite a statement, "All Scripture." First, if that is true, we know specifically that God made his creation, not in a "god-of-the-gaps" way, but with purpose, love, and grandeur:

> "For since the creation of the world His invisible *attributes, that is,* His eternal power and divine nature, have been clearly perceived, being

understood by what has been made, so that they are without excuse.

Romans 1:20

"Oh, Lord God! Behold, You Yourself have made the heavens and the earth by Your great power and by Your outstretched arm! Nothing is too difficult for You"

Jeremiah 32:17

"By the word of the Lord the heavens were made, And by the breath of His mouth all their lights.

Psalm 33:6

"All things came into being through Him, and apart from Him not even one thing came into being that has come into being."

John 1:3

"For You created my innermost parts; You wove me in my mother's womb."

Psalm 139:13

God's word speaks specifically to all aspects of a worldview including who we are and we come from. It provides us purpose, moral guidance, and of course meaning and ultimately, an understanding of our destiny, which is to be with him forever, in a new heaven and earth, with a new, glorified body far removed from the effects or the potential for sin. Outspoken atheists have not only ignored the Bible, but they have taken it head-on, although out of context and brutally inaccurate. The fact is atheists who subscribe to naturalism or materialism only use the Bible out of context to argue against God rather than trying to learn theology or, more specifically, hermeneutics, which is the art and science of biblical interpretation.

However, even when readers do not take the extreme approach that Dawkins or other atheists make, some may still ask, "How in the world can we trust a book written so long ago by so many different people?" And what about all of the commands, the do's and don'ts, and all of the massacres and violence? And let's not forget, according to Richard Dawkins and other outspoken atheists, the Bible condones slavery, misogyny, infanticide, murder, and just about every other form of reprehensible act you would likely find in a graphic novel.

Furthermore, the argument has been made, "If the God of the Bible does exist, I want no part of him!" Of course, the outspoken Richard Dawkins is front and center on attacks against the Bible. Prominent atheists have taken on the Bible at great lengths in bits and pieces because they see religion as a great evil in society and any doctrine or belief involving religion is going to be a target for vehement dissent. However, with that said, the Bible claims to be divinely inspired, so what is the evidence that the Bible is inspired or God-breathed. Also, how do we account for the God of the Bible if it is truly inspired? Several passages appear troubling when examined at first glance or on a superficial level.

Answering Assertions

One of the most common assertions made against the Bible is that it condones slavery. Of course, America's troubled history with slavery creates feelings of anger and confusion when read in the pages of the Bible by someone who is not familiar with what is called "ancient near-eastern" (ANE) traditions. The Bible does not promote ethnic slavery. There were indentured servants, fellow Israelites who had become indebted to others for financial reasons. There were also captured enemies as a result of war. While it is true that plantation and slave owners in the American south used the Bible to justify slavery in their own corrupt belief system, a brief analysis will reveal that biblical references were taken well out of context. Slaveholders who, I would argue, were ignorant of biblical theology themselves and failed to acknowledge the Image of God in their slaves. In the Bible acts of cruelty against an indentured slave resulted in instant freedom. Moreover, southern slaveholders certainly did not set their slaves free on the seventh year, or Jubilee, as tied to the Sabbath and was customary in Levitical Law.

Another frequent reference in the Old Testament is that of warfare when God command's the Israelites to kill all of the men, women, and children in what Richard Dawkins uses to call God "genocidal, homicidal, infanticidal...." The Canaanite people were not only possessing the Promised Land but they were also being judged for their horrific evil against their own people. The Canaanites were historically guilty of sacrificing infants and children on molten hot idols, specifically to their god *Molek*. The Canaanites were dangerous, violent people, and Israel, at times, was prone to fall into the practices of these corrupt nations. Leviticus 20:2 speaks of God commanding that any Israelite who is caught sacrificing their child to *Molek* was to be stoned to death. Such a harsh sentence is of course not only for the murder of innocent life but for attempting to lead the nation of Israel into pagan worship despite the amazing revelation God revealed to them since their deliverance from Egypt.

Again, such a topic requires significant study and research from a variety of different sources, some have also suggested that ancient practices of hyperbole are most correctly used to interpret the command in Scripture to, "kill everything that breaths." Studying Scripture under historical contexts of ancient Israel, especially in communication styles and genres, can help us understand what Scot McKnight is writing when he explains,

"No longer is the object of Israel's warfare against the Canaanites to kill (literally) every man, woman, and child, combatant and noncombatant alike, as many readers have thought. Rather, the conquest of Canaan meant defeating the Canaanite armies in battle and driving out of the land at least a significant portion of the Canaanite population.[1]

Hyperbole has been defined as "when more is said than is meant."[2] There are examples of hyperbole in both the Old and New Testaments. When Jesus tells someone to take the log out of their eye before they remove a speck from their brother's eye. Moreover, Scripture verses referring to "all the people" in instances of public actions or responses in some cases are cases of hyperbole. Hyperbole was common in these ancient cultures and writings and in some cases, if I stated that I typed the pages of this book until my fingers fell off, you would understand the nuances of hyperbole today. It is simply used as a way to communicate strong emphases.

Imprecatory prayers or Psalms can be another point of contention for someone who picks up the Bible to read it as if they were reading a novel or the Sunday newspaper. In an emotional appeal to the audience, one atheist started off a debate with Dr. Frank Turek by reading Psalm 137:9, *"Blessed will be the one who seizes and dashes your children against the rocks."* This of course was an emotional appeal that the atheist used, and a method that has been used by other atheists in debates, as well as in written literature, arguing against the validity of the Bible. However, a deeper look into this Psalm, with the help of biblical scholars, helps the reader to understand that the Psalmist was singing a song written when Israel was forced to sing to the Babylonians while marching into captivity into modern-day Iraq after Israel had been completely destroyed by them, including having their children murdered and, most likely, babies smashed into rocks by these very same Babylonians.

The final assertion that will be addressed, although there are others levied by atheists, is that women were treated with disdain and as property throughout the Bible. Regardless of what the condition was after the fall and in the growing pains of Israel as a nation being delivered from bondage, the biblical understanding of the role of women can be found in no greater place than in Genesis 2:18-22, women are the image of God and have the same ontological value as a man. There are two distinctions of women, as described in one commentary as for the word "helper" as "a help, a counterpart of himself, one formed from him, and a perfect resemblance of his person. If the word is to be rendered literally, it signifies one *like*, or as *himself*, standing *opposite to* or *before him*.[3]

The Hebrew words for the woman as the helper are *Ezer Kenegdo* and these words also have a context for summoning for help in a military sense and the word is again used to refer to a rescuer in a summons to God. Consider that God did not create Eve right beside Adam after putting him to sleep. Eve was created apart from Adam as God himself brought Eve to Adam as a divine magisterial gift over all creation. One might consider that this divine act had the highest intent for the role that woman was to play in the life of man and that certainly is not one of subservience but of co-regency with him.

In the New Testament, we find women were the first witnesses of Jesus' resurrection, although Jewish law would not permit women to testify on their own in a civil proceeding. When you read through the Gospels you will find men, including the disciples, who did not believe Jesus, who abandoned him, and who rejected him. There is not one recorded event of women in the Gospels doing anything but offering reverence, faith, or support to Jesus. The Apostle Paul makes references to women in his ministry leading in churches and risking their very lives to help him. Regardless of the failures of society, and there are many, the divine mandate for women is established when one becomes a student of Scripture, which atheists rarely do in cases where they seek to reference a single verse of Scripture with no context to make an argument.

Examples such as these are emotional appeals by some atheists to get others to hate or despise theism as they do. There has been dialogue with apologists who have asked atheists, "If the Bible were proven to be true, would you become a Christian?" and to their credit, most of the time they answer, "No." Atheists want people to embrace emotional appeals to elementary arguments against the existence of God or the truthfulness of Scripture, but they either have never examined the evidence themselves or are just too hardhearted to accept any evidence and they will only feel better about their miserable state when someone agrees with them on this issue.

Digging for Truth

There is a tremendous amount of history in the Bible. Key people, places, and events are inundated throughout the historical narratives within the Bible. At times, questions and doubts have been expressed by historians concerning key historical claims within the Bible. However, in the last century, amazing archaeological discoveries have been found not only in Israel but throughout the Middle East, particularly in Egypt, that validates biblical records as historically accurate. Again, many discoveries countered claims from critics and liberal scholars about the veracity of biblical accuracy.

Biblical Archaeology Review reports that more than fifty significant people listed in the Bible have been confirmed to have been a historical figure through archaeological discoveries.[4] The names found in archaeological excavations include kings, rulers, and key people in Old Testament history. Moreover, archaeology has also verified key locations in the Bible as well as times and eras. One unique discovery was related to the first of two events in history where Jerusalem was destroyed. A twenty-two-foot tower, twelve feet deep with ashes at its base as well as arrowheads from Israel and the Babylonians from the siege in 589 B.C. This is the same incident of when the Israelites were carried off into captivity (as mentioned in reference to the imprecatory Psalm 137:9 earlier in this chapter).

Perhaps the most intriguing find was the Dead Sea Scrolls which were dated three hundred years before Christ. The Dead Sea Scrolls contain fragments from every book of the Old Testament except the Book of Esther.[5] When compared with the second oldest manuscripts, dated more than one thousand years later, the documents were virtually identical. The Hebrew Scriptures were preserved with exquisite detail because of their love and reverence for the *Tanakh*, but in the same way, New Testament letters were copied and distributed in the first century after Christ. While no one is asserting that copies are 100% identical from the original source document, which we no longer have, with almost 6,000 partial and complete copies of New Testament documents available for critical examination,[6] there are critical approaches to ensure the integrity of the overall source.

What is also important to understand about biblical archaeology is that there are no contradictions between archaeological finds and biblical narratives. Some of the leading experts in biblical archaeology with decades of experience in Middle East excavations and studies have made some profound statements concerning biblical accuracy verified through archaeological sites. Here is what just a small number of experts have said regarding their experience in biblical archaeology:[7]

> "It may be stated categorically that no archaeological discovery has ever controverted a Biblical reference. Scores of archaeological findings have been made which confirm in clear outline or exact detail historical statements in the Bible. And, by the same token, proper evaluation of Biblical description has often led to amazing discoveries."

Dr. Nelson Glueck,
The Renowned Jewish Archeologist.

"Archaeology has confirmed countless passages which have been rejected by critics as unhistorical or contradictory to known 'facts'."

Dr. Joseph Free

"There can be no doubt that archaeology has confirmed the substantial historicity of Old Testament tradition."

Dr. William F. Albright,

"The great value of archaeology has been to show, over and over again, that the geography, technology, political and military movements, cultures, religious practices, social institutions, languages, customs, and other aspects of everyday life of Israel and other nations of antiquity were exactly as described in the Bible."

Dr. Henry M. Morris

...Archeological work has unquestionably strengthened confidence in the reliability of the scriptural record. More than one archeologist has found respect for the Bible increased by the experience of excavation in Palestine.

Millar Burrows, Yale archaeologist

Predicting the Future

Imagine if you will a letter that you receive in the mail and on it is written: "Do Not Open Until You Get to Work tomorrow!"

Unlike me, you have some level of patience and you decide to do just that as your curiosity spikes. As soon as you try to start your car the next morning, your battery is dead. You start to call AAA and your Uncle Ned drives by and sees that you need a battery jump and gets you on the road. You go to Starbucks and your favorite flavor is not available so you decide to just get a Grande Hot Chocolate. When you finally get to your office you sit down and start to drink your beverage and you finally open the envelope and it reads. "Your car battery will be dead, but you will get help from Uncle Ned. Are you enjoying your hot chocolate from Starbucks? By the way, during your meeting, you are going to spill the hot chocolate on your boss's budget reports and get fired on the spot.

There are two primary ways to look at this scenario... random chance or something strange is in the mix. So, do you take your hot chocolate into the meeting with your boss to go over the budget reports or do you leave it on your desk considering three things that happened this morning that could not have been planned out without Uncle Ned and the Barista being involved, unless your Uncle Ned is the Barista at Starbucks and he ran down your battery? For most people, such a letter would have a bone-chilling effect and we would leave our hot chocolate at our desk just to be safe. In this scenario, you would be deciding your financial future based on three predictions that came true that were predicted only one day before the event. Of course, this is an extreme example, but when we read the Bible, we can find that there were twenty-seven prophesies fulfilled just on the day that Jesus was crucified that were written hundreds of years before Christ (remember, the *Dead Sea Scrolls* put at least 300 years between the prophecies and the birth and death of Jesus).[8] Ps 41:9 Even my own close friend in whom I trusted, who ate my bread, has lifted up *his* heel against me.

- *(Fulfilled) Mark 14:10 Then Judas Iscariot, who was one of the twelve, went off to the chief priests in order to betray Him to them.*

Zech 13:7 "Awake, O sword, against My Shepherd, Against the Man who is My Associate," Declares the Lord of armies. "Strike the Shepherd, and the sheep will be scattered; And I will turn My hand against the little ones."

- *(Fulfilled) Mark 14:50 And His disciples all left Him and fled.*

Zech 11:12 Then I said to them, "If it is good in your sight, give *me* my wages; and if not, never mind." So, they weighed out thirty shekels of silver as my wages.

- *(Fulfilled) Matthew 26:14-15 Then one of the twelve, named Judas Iscariot, went unto the chief priests, and said, what are you willing to give me, to betray him to you? And they set out for him thirty pieces of silver.*

Isa 50:6 I gave My back to those who strike Me, And My cheeks to those who pull out my beard; I did not hide My face from insults and spitting.

- *(Fulfilled) Mathew 27:26, 30 Then he released Barabbas for them; but after having Jesus flogged, he handed Him to be crucified… And they spit on Him, and took the reed and beat Him on the head.*

Ps 22:18 They divide My garments among them, and they cast lots for My clothing.

- *(Fulfilled) John 19:24 So they said to one another, "Let's not tear it, but cast lots for it, to decide whose it shall be." This happened so that the Scripture would be fulfilled: "THEY DIVIDED MY GARMENTS AMONG THEMSELVES, AND THEY CAST LOTS FOR MY CLOTHING." Therefore, the soldiers did these things.*

Isa 53:7 He was oppressed and afflicted, Yet He did not open His mouth;
Like a lamb that is led to slaughter, And like a sheep that is silent before its shearers,
So He did not open His mouth.

- (Fulfilled) Matthew 27:13-14 *Then Pilate said to Him, "Do You not hear how many things they are testifying against You?" And still He did not answer him regarding a single charge, so the governor was greatly amazed.*

Ps 69:21 They also gave me a bitter herb in my food, and for my thirst, they gave me vinegar to drink.

- (Fulfilled) *John 19:29 A jar full of sour wine was standing there; so they put a sponge full of the sour wine on a branch of hyssop and brought it up to His mouth.*

Ps 22:16 For dogs have surrounded Me; A band of evildoers has encompassed Me. They pierced My hands and My feet.

- (Fulfilled) Matthew 27:35 *And when they crucified Him, they divided His garments among themselves, casting lots.*

Isa 53:9 And His grave was assigned with wicked men, Yet He was with a rich man in His death, Because He had done no violence, Nor was there any deceit in His mouth.

- *(Fulfilled) Matthew 27:57-60 Now when it was evening, a rich man from Arimathea came, named Joseph, who himself had also become a disciple of Jesus. This man went to Pilate and asked for the body of Jesus. Then Pilate ordered it to be given to him. And Joseph took the body and wrapped it in a clean linen cloth, and laid it in his own new tomb, which he had cut out in the rock; and he rolled a large stone against the entrance of the tomb and went away.*

When you consider the inspiration of Scripture you must consider that the Holy Spirit acted upon writers who were men, but who were inspired to write by God. Islam believes in direct word-for-word dictation in the Koran and Mormons believe that their (false) prophet used a seer-stone to dictate new revelations to the church. However, the writers in the Bible who wrote as they were moved by the Holy Spirit possessed uncanny accuracy and detail in the times of Ancient Israel and the first-century church. The evidence that they were inspired is not only in archaeology, fulfilled prophecy but also in the honest details and facts by which people of the Bible who were trying to follow God failed miserably. Embarrassing details such Abraham lying to save his life, David's adulterous affair, Peter's Cowardice, and so many other leadership, moral and other failures as implicated in the Scripture.

Examining the Evidence: 🔍

The Bible is the Word of God. Not a lot the Word of God, not even mostly the Word of God, but divinely inspired. The fact that we struggle to grasp it at times and can even be frustrated with the content does not change that, nor does it make you a bad person. The God who made the heavens and the earth, and breathed life into humanity has chosen to communicate to us in a way that is just as miraculous as our DNA or the perfect order of the laws in our universe. The message that is communicated quite simply is, "You are my people, and I love you, and I will redeem you to myself."

The Bible is not a list of commands, or do's and don'ts. When God's people were brought out of Egypt they had 613 commands, but Jesus told his disciples there are only two commands. First, "To love the Lord your God with all your heart, all your soul, and all your mind." This book was written to help you do just that, especially with the aspect of your mind or doubts that you may have about God, or his purpose or plan for you. And second, "To love your neighbor as yourself." How could such a message be the target of vehement rhetoric and hatred? Because the Bible is divinely inspired, it is going to be the target of debate and dissension, especially from those who despise God's Word and lack the effort to actually study the Bible in a manner that even closely compares to their academic discipline.

If someone is looking to disprove the Bible, they are going to have to do so on their own because the evidence is overwhelming that this amazing book is exactly what it says. If you struggle with belief, begin with prayer as you open and also as you read through the text. Again, find resources that are credible as there is a lot of bad information available that is either unhealthy or heretical movements such as the *Word-Faith Movement*, Jehovah's Witnesses, Mormons, and any host of aberrant faith-based groups that assault the integrity and alter the message of God's Word.

"For my thoughts are not your thoughts, nor are your ways My ways, declares the Lord"

Isaiah 55:8

9   Miracles

Atheistic challenges to the phenomena of miracles in historic Christianity are often only a secondary objection to theism that typically falls in line with the personal attacks involving the nature of God or the intellectual level of theists. The argument that atheists present against the possibility of miracles is that our universe and our world is a closed system regarding the physical laws of nature. To successfully argue this point, the key assumptions must be held that everything in our universe can be reduced to matter and energy. Every cause-and-effect is in a closed loop with no real beginning. These assumptions have already been addressed in prior chapters e.g., *Mind vs. Matter, Flaws and Faith*, but as in many arguments, the limited scope of atheist objections can be challenged on multiple fronts, especially within the context of worldview analysis.

One of the key historical figures that atheists refer to in their claims against the phenomena of miracles is the eighteenth century philosopher David Hume. Hume is noted for his works in empiricism and skepticism, of which the phenomenon of miracles centers well upon. Hume writes on the historical evidence for miracles being insufficient when compared to the human sensory experiences,

> *"Our evidence, then, for the truth of the Christian religion is less than the evidence for the truth of our senses, because even in the first authors of our religion it was no greater; and it is evident it must*

diminish in passing from them to their disciples, nor can anyone rest such confidence in their testimony as in the immediate object of his senses. But a weaker evidence can never destroy a stronger; and, therefore, were the doctrine of the real presence ever so clearly revealed in scripture, it would be directly contrary to the rules of just reasoning to give our assent to it."[1]

Hume's primary argument is that no evidence or eye-witness testimony would be sufficient to accept the occurrence of a miracle because that evidence falls beneath the confidence and certainty our sense experiences. Hume argues that evidence in support of miracles should not even be examined because whatever evidence is discovered will still not be enough to convince anyone of miracles. Interestingly enough, atheists, especially scientists like Dawkins, accuse someone who has a Christian worldview of being superstitious and refusing to look intellectually into the world. In other words, atheists argue that believing in God necessarily requires one to stop scientific inquiry and just say, "God did it." However, it is Hume who is saying, do not bother investigating claims of miracles, because they cannot happen. Even if you establish evidence that a miracle did happen it will not rise to the level of the senses. Hume's argument for the absolute certainty of the senses, we find, is even susceptible under philosophical scrutiny.

More than a century earlier, Hume's pragmatic approach to certainty through the senses was previously acknowledged by Rene Descartes to be subject to vulnerability in what was titled, "the error of the senses." Descartes argued, "The senses deceive from time to time, and it's prudent never to trust wholly those who have deceived us once before."[2] An oasis in the desert from someone suffering from the effects of extreme temperatures or dehydrated shipwrecked sailors believing saltwater is fresh, and there are the classroom scientific experiments with perceptions of a pencil or straw being disjointed when looked at from angles in a clear glass of water.

Of course, we can trust our senses as long as they have not been compromised, but Hume's conclusions are most accurate for the natural laws that occur every day, and we would be correct to put extreme confidence in our experiences and observations. We can overcome a fear of flying by observing aircraft taking off and landing at a large airport without incident or fear of the water by watching swimmers in the water without being attacked by a shark or drowning. Hume and Descartes both have valid arguments involving sensory experience, but their arguments are best applied to a physical world with a closed system and do little to explain the potential for miracles.

In the Gospel of John, we read of one of the disciples, Thomas, who embraced Hume's reasoning from the human senses. After the resurrection of Jesus, the disciples informed Thomas of their post-resurrection encounter with Jesus and Thomas responded to their claims, "Unless I touch the wounds on his hands and in his side, I will not believe." Thomas rejected narratives of the resurrected Lord unless the event could be confirmed by his sensory experience. Although Thomas's senses were working, he refused to accept the news of Jesus' resurrection by testimony. Jesus had even referenced his death and resurrection when he was with disciples. Jesus' response to Thomas was the acknowledgment of his faith-based upon him seeing but told him that those who believe who have not seen him (physically) would be blessed. Again, Jesus is not expecting people to have blind faith in him, but one that is evidence-based, in part, on the historical narrative of the miracles that followed his teaching.

Miracles or Myths

In critiquing a worldview that includes the existence of miracles we should look through the Bible to understand the context and purpose for the existence of miracles. Hume's argument is that miracles cannot exist so historical reports that they did occur must be assumed to either be the product of misperception or deception. There are well over one hundred miracles recorded in the Bible beginning with creation through the works of the disciples after Christ ascended into heaven. When reading Scripture, it should be understood that the terms "signs" and "wonders" are often used together and sometimes interchangeably when recording miraculous events. These events are often used to confirm messages from God through individuals inspired by the Holy Spirit.

John 20:30 records that *"Jesus did many other signs in the presence of the disciples, which are not written in this book, but these have been written so that you might believe."* John fully intended his readers to grasp the veracity of miracles centered on the person and the works of Jesus Christ. The recordings in the Gospels, of course, were preceded by oral traditions that were most likely already written in some form of creed. In the book of *1 Corinthians*, the Apostle Paul references doctrinal information in the historical reference to Jesus Christ,

> *"For I handed down to you as of first importance what I also received, that Christ died for our sins according to the Scriptures, and that He was buried, and that He was raised on the third day according to the Scriptures, and that He appeared to Cephas, then to the twelve. After that He appeared to more than five hundred brothers and sisters at one time, most of whom remain until now, but some have fallen asleep; then He appeared to James, then to*

> *all the apostles; and last of all, as to one untimely*
> *born, He appeared to me also...."*
>
> 1 Corinthians 15:3-8

The miracles of Jesus, in this case, his death and resurrection, are inundated within the first-century church by eyewitnesses who proclaimed these truths in the midst of severe persecution. The witness accounts and oral history of the miracles around Jesus' earthly ministry took place in Jerusalem and surrounding cities with an extreme population density.[3] News of his ministry gathered momentum because it not only involved the supernatural in a highly dense population with strong oral communication but also, disrupted the ruling religious and ruling elite. Jewish sources such as *Josephus* and the Roman historian *Tacitus* made historical references to Jesus. It defies logic to argue that the historical Jesus, who had a ministry in this geographically confined area with a large population, would have amassed such an amazing following, but for the presence of miracles in addition to his teaching as one with authority.

Jesus Christ was betrayed because he rejected the idea of an actual revolt against the oppressive Roman Empire. He was arrested and tried because he claimed to be one with God, claims that can be easily supported with even a basic understanding of theology and biblical Greek. Ultimately, three years after he sat upon a mountain and began to teach the beatitudes to the masses, he was executed as a criminal, according to false testimony and the result of a secret, illegal court held in the dark, early morning hours instead of in the day according to Jewish law. Why would a man who had a three-year ministry and amazing teaching but who had never healed anyone or performed any miracles have to be executed in the dark of night away from the public?

Was Jesus simply a phenomenal orator? In the *Book of John*, Nicodemus, a Pharisee, and member of the Sanhedrin, pays a visit to Jesus under the cover of night to acknowledge that Jesus is a teacher come from God because no man can do these signs that he does unless God is with him. Keep in mind, if Jesus Christ performed even one genuine miracle, including his virgin birth, the entire argument against the possibility of supernatural phenomenon collapses under the weight of truth. The *Gospel of John* also records that after Jesus' death, Nicodemus and Joseph of Arimathea came out in open support of Jesus at his crucifixion to purchase a place to bury him. The prophecy of Jesus being "lifted up (on a cross) and drawing all men unto me" is immediately coming to fulfillment as these two prominent Jewish men openly show support of Christ.[4]

The miracles that have been recorded in the *Torah*, many of which were performed through God at the hand of Moses, are in the dozens. Is Moses a liar? Was he so disillusioned while walking in the wilderness as to confuse a burning bush speaking with him with some other natural phenomena? Was it the voices in his own head that told him to abandon his life and take on the most powerful military leader known at that time? Again, if even one of the dozens of miracles that were recorded in the Jewish Scriptures occurred the entire argument that we are in a closed system is proven false.

So, to the atheist, the question is posed, "Are the historical figures in the Bible liars or lunatics?" The sacred preservation of Scripture within the Jewish and early Christian traditions was beyond reproach in capturing key people, places, and events with the only surviving people-group to still exist today from that geographical area known as modern-day Israel. The prophet Isaiah asked in prophetic prose, "*Who has heard such a thing? Who has seen such things? Can a land be born in one day? Can a nation be given birth all at once? As soon as Zion was in labor, she also delivered her sons.*" (Isaiah 66:8), May 14, 1948, the nation of Israel was reborn after disappearing for almost two thousand years and the Jewish people came out of the four corners of the earth (*hyperbole*) to come home. There is absolutely no nation or people group even close to fulfilling such an amazing feat. Israel is a nation of miracles and there is more to come.

Resurrection of Jesus

The physical resurrection of Jesus Christ has been a matter of contention from the day that it occurred. The ebb and flow of academic dissention in modern times is well recorded in modern debate. Multiple theories have been postulated that Jesus did not really die on the cross. There was the *swoon theory* that Jesus just collapsed and was only presumed dead when they took him off the cross. Keep in mind that he would have had to have fully recovered in a cave without treatment when medical experts today would argue that the best emergency room would not have been able to have saved Jesus after coming off the cross had he not been dead.

The *hallucination theory* incorporated a mass, coordinated psychiatric malady insisting on Jesus' resurrection and, of course, there's the "let's hide the body and go to our execution insisting Jesus rose from the dead" theory. All of the disciples except for John, who was tortured and died on *Patmos* (after writing the *Book of Revelation*) were not only tortured but executed for their faith, for what they believed in… a resurrected Christ. Suffice it to say, there have been prolific conversations on the resurrection of the dead as it should be as a central tenet of the Christian faith. Without the resurrection, there can be no Christianity.

The Apostle Paul said in *1 Corinthians 15:14* *"and if Christ has not been raised, then our preaching is in vain, your faith also is in vain."* The resurrection of Jesus Christ is arguably the greatest miracle in the Bible considering there is some astonishing evidence for this historic event that is significantly greater than arguments against the person and resurrection of Jesus. Only a select amount of information in a summary form can be presented here, but leading theologians in the area of the resurrection, including Gary Habermas of Liberty University, are cited and serve as a resource for further reading. Habermas' Ph.D. dissertation speaks to the theological, historical, and philosophical tenets of the resurrection of Jesus Christ. Habermas' historical references will be the only approach here in providing some response to atheists, including that the logic of Hume would discount any narrative that is contrary to the human sensory experience.

The death of Jesus Christ is widely accepted as a historical fact even among non-Christian and liberal circles. However, in the battle of worldviews, the resurrection of Jesus is still a mildly fortified position since skeptics have fallen back to that argument almost exclusively in defense against the supernatural. There are multiple historical vantage points from which to argue for the physical and literal resurrection of Jesus Christ and from these vantage points come several assertions concerning the historical accuracy of the resurrection. As the historical arguments for the resurrection of Jesus Christ mount, the only target of opportunity for atheists, or anyone who denies the supernatural event of the resurrection, is to attack the evidence, namely the Gospels and New Testament, or the disciples themselves. There are aspiring atheists who have taken the time and effort to present blogs and webpages to invite dialogue or debate on the resurrection, but many of these sites cover arguments that have already faded into the historical sunset.

The empty tomb stands out as perhaps the most glaring evidence in support of the resurrection of Christ. There are no shrines, which are typical of famous deceased leaders, and there was no body. If the Romans, religious leaders, and anyone who opposed Jesus Christ simply presented the badly beaten and deformed body of a dead man from Nazareth there would have been no movement and certainly no first-century church that grew exponentially so quickly after the event. Some historians have concluded that careful, unprejudiced study of the historical evidence is said to lead either to absolute certainty about the resurrection, or at least to a conviction of its overwhelming plausibility.[5] In either way, the evidence is far more likely than not from a position of inquiry that the empty tomb was the result of Jesus walking out after being raised from the dead – a miracle by anyone's standard.

Life-After-Death

Perhaps if atheists cannot argue against the resurrection of Jesus Christ, they can mount an argument against life after death for those of us without a divine nature. Atheists claim that there is no life after death because they are, for the most part, strict naturalists. If the material world is all that there ever was, is, or ever will be, there can be no such thing as an after-life. Moreover, any such evidence for life after death would be classified as supernatural or a miracle if a human being could demonstrate evidence of consciousness and awareness after medical doctors proclaimed that person clinically dead.

There is a lot of information on the topic of life-after-death events, also referred to as near-death experiences or NDEs. As with any resource, any information taken for consumption needs to be evaluated and carefully examined within the context of professional or peer-reviewed literature. One such resource is *The Journal for Near-Death Studies*, a quarterly research journal that only considers NDEs that meet specific criteria that facilitate the collection of data and other relevant information. The Journal of Near-Death-Experiences is not a publication to prove that God exists or validates any religion, it is a scientific journal that examines evidence of consciousness after clinical death occurs in a hospital setting.

Currently, *The Journal of NDE* has more than 1,100 NDE cases in their research, but none as intriguing as individuals who experienced an NDE and who were also blind from birth. Research suggests that congenitally blind people do not experience visual sensation when they dream, having not attained visualization of imagery in the physical world, but rather, experienced the world through sounds, smells, and other sensory channels. There are references of congenitally blind people having "virtual images,"[6] but that term was not been sufficiently defined, although the context appears to indicate that *virtual* implies imagery developed from other senses. The Journal of NDE currently has just over 30 cases involving blind NDEs, 14 of those cases involved patients who were blind from birth. The case studies revealed that the NDE experiences were identical to people who were not visually impaired or blind people who lost their vision later on in life.[7]

One of the more unique cases within the congenitally blind group is the research involving Vicki Umping and Brad Barrows. Vicki and Brad experienced NDEs, also referred to in the research as Out-of-Body-Experiences (OBEs), and experienced perfect vision that was later described in detail, including vision spanning 360°. They described people, places, weather, and of course, their encounter in heaven of loved ones and Jesus himself. Again, in this context, this research is merely trying to present the scientific evidence, through scientific inquiry, that people who were born blind, who have never visually observed a person, a tree, or any other object, who reportedly dream with only the sense experience of sound, smell, and feeling, and are certainly not capable of describing people present in rooms when they died, did exactly that based on scientific inquiry and fact-finding involving non-biased interviews and evidence collection that validated their testimony.

Examining the Evidence: 🔍

We understand that there is significant evidence for the truth and veracity of the Bible. Archaeological evidence of people, places, and events provide pristine support of the Bible's accuracy and commitment to reporting truth, even when that reporting taints the image of important people who did not quite live up to their expectation at times. According to one faith-based website, it is calculated more than 80 miracles occurred in the Old Testament and 80 known miracles occurred in the New Testament. If even one of those miracles as reported in the Bible is true then the conclusion must be made that miracles do occur and we do not live in a closed system where God or the supernatural does not intervene at times.

Foremost, the evidence for the resurrection of Jesus Christ is overwhelming and the fact is that the first century church grew exponentially even as disciples and many other followers were tortured and murdered without relenting from their faith. They were ordinary people with fears and doubts, people who had nothing to gain by lying about the resurrection of Jesus, but whose lives were completely changed. Two thousand years later we are debating the significance of the person and the works of Jesus Christ and the people who followed him. As a figure of history and faith, the person of Jesus Christ exceeds the relevance of anyone in history and he never took up a sword or a weapon, he never hurt anyone or advocated violence. He simply entered our world with a message, *"Repent, for the Kingdom of Heaven is at hand." And for that, he is hated above all men.*

10 Evil and Suffering

The greatest objection to the existence of God is the presence of evil and suffering in our world, sometimes referred to in philosophical circles as *The Problem of Evil.* The problem of evil and suffering is the most difficult question theist must respond to in efforts to justify the existence of an all-loving and all-powerful God. It is one thing to consider the philosophical question of evil and suffering and it is completely another to be experiencing the immense pain that is so often associated with significant loss or tragedy and the question "Why?" The philosophical question of the problem of evil will be addressed in this chapter, although admittedly, not sufficiently. However, if you are reading this book and you are going through an experience of intense pain or suffering there are no words to address the "why" question. Honestly, it would be insufficient or perhaps even offensive to attempt to explain in philosophical terms the *what* or the *why* of your experience.

The effort to try and bring some light on a very dark and difficult subject is not intended to trivialize the reality of suffering in the world that causes some to conclude there cannot be a god if X, Y, or Z happens. It has already been referenced of the level of pain and suffering that many well-known atheists have experienced, specifically the loss of a parent at a young age or being subjected to intense physical or emotional abuse by a loved one. There is often little logic in the process of grief and suffering. There is the hopeful presence of those who mean so much to us and the assurance that there is something more glorious that awaits us that the Apostle Paul summarized in Romans 8:18, in that these present sufferings were not even comparable to the glory that will be revealed to us [for all eternity]. *Emphasis added.*

The problem of evil, within the context of the Judeo-Christian worldview, is called a "theodicy." A theodicy is a philosophical approach to justify the existence of God in light of the presence of evil. In the movie *Man of Steel*, the character of Lex Luther brought up the philosophical question that argued against God in our world, "If God is all-powerful, he cannot be all good. And if he is all good, then he cannot be all-powerful." Luther of course takes this philosophical paradox from the Greek philosopher *Epicurus*. Now, one can argue that atheism does not prove that God cannot exist in a world with evil, and atheists certainly have no standard for "good" without God, but still, this argument falls short of seeking to argue for the existence of God in a positive way. Remember, in the grand scheme of the worldview, you must ask which explanation between atheism and theism provides the most consistent and reliable response to our world, not just explaining the physical status, but the moral one as well.

A logical line of consistency should be pursued to engage this challenging question, if not to answer the problem, to at least bring some clarity in light of the reality of the problem of evil and suffering as contained within a Christian worldview. The question is then, "What do we do with a belief system that cannot provide all of the answers that we want in our worldview?" You can still maintain a Christian worldview with both logical and internal consistency even if you cannot completely address a complex philosophical problem, especially one that has been addressed by great intellectuals over more than two millennia. For example, in the field of mathematics, there are many problems that are seemingly "unsolvable," but mathematicians do not abandon their field in light of problems that cannot be reconciled through theory or fully extrapolated. In all honestly, perhaps one day these mathematical problems will be solved through continued development, or perhaps artificial intelligence, but the problem of evil will never be completely resolved this side of the new heaven and the new earth that is referenced in the final chapter of the book of Revelation.

Atheistic Pretentions

The pain and anger that the late Christopher Hitchens and Sam Harris described when the terrorists flew passenger aircraft into the Twin Towers were not unique to atheists, but perhaps their disdain for all religion was, or at least pretty close, to being unique. Atheists such as Dawkins and Harris take an inductive approach to religion in that specific acts throughout history done in the name of religion should be applied to all religions. They make a general conclusion based on specific observations such as terrorism. Richard Dawkins believes that religion is a "force of evil" and "a virus that is passed down through generations."[1]

Richard Dawkins takes great steps to argue religion as a force of evil and references the evil acts committed by atheist leaders as only coincidental. Dawkins acknowledges the reality that the twentieth century's two worst dictators were atheists, namely Stalin and Hitler. However, Dawkins is quick to conclude from his logical summary that "there is not the smallest evidence that atheism motivated Stalin's brutality.[2] Having studied and taught military history as a former intelligence officer, it is understood that military strategy involves understanding every facet of geopolitical leaders – their decision-making trends, inability to delegate authority, and of course, who these individuals are as people and what is important to them. Marxism was at the core of Josef Stalin's motivation; it was the theoretical ideal to the revolutionary violence that had him arrested decades prior.

Dawkins also failed to acknowledge the extreme atheist rhetoric within Marxism, later developed through the work of

Hegel and Ludwig Feuerbach who wrote that belief in the God of Christianity leads "to a belief in revelation and sacraments which are items of an undesirable religious materigism."[3] In fact, Dawkins and Marx have the identical starting point in their critique of problems in society having the role of religion serving as the root cause. Karl Marx believed that the starting point of what was wrong with society begins with the criticism of religion, although politics and economics were also included in a world system that needed to be completely overturned.[4]

Richard Dawkins ponders the wrong question from a philosophical vantage point. He asks if atheism systematically influences people to do bad things. Of course, the answer is "no" among people. There are very good, moral people who believe that there is no God and no afterlife, but Dawkins misrepresents the significance of Stalin and Hitler because these men did not believe they were doing bad things, but rather, they believed that they were doing good things and the foundation for this belief, especially for Hitler, was a worldview with naturalism and evolution at its very core. Belief in God was a manmade construct, and its only purpose is to hinder the evolution of man, not surprisingly, yet another argument that Richard Dawkins makes for the case of atheism. To Dawkins, Darwinian evolution is the vehicle by which to move humanity forward and religion is like a "virus" that needs to be eradicated from being passed down through generations.

Whether this foundation of materialism lies with Marxist ideology or Darwinian evolution, the calling for mankind to shed the negative effects of religion and to grasp a higher intellectual struggle is without much distinction. People in authority who subscribe to a view of humanity that falls short of the Christian doctrine, which mandates a view of mankind being created in God's image, have unlimited potential to engage in dangerous behavior. As the Milgram Experiment demonstrates, if someone can find a thread of good in even the most extreme behavior, the potential for human evil becomes much greater than we would like to believe.

German colonies in Africa committed acts of genocide against the *Herero* and *Nama* people, killing an estimated 50 to 80 percent of their population, all in the name of Social Darwinism.[5] Darwinian evolution and the laws of natural selection served as justification for extermination and all-out war as a biological necessity for survival of the fittest. Of course, these views were promulgated by Darwin himself, in part, through his publishing of the *Descent of Man* which he wrote, "At some future period, not very distant as measured by centuries, the civilized races of man will almost certainly exterminate and replace throughout the world the savage races."[6] The embracing of Darwinian evolution permeated Germany's political, social, and academic circles.

General Lothar von Trotha, the field commander for the German Army responsible for the genocide, was quoted as saying, "human feelings of philanthropy could not override the law of Darwin's the struggle of the fittest."[7] Ultimately, the acts of these social elites felt external pressure, and the Herero and Nama people were moved to concentration camps as part of a less obvious extermination effort. Unfortunately, the direct link between the Social Darwinian with this horrific crime, the first act of genocide in the twentieth century, cannot be found in Internet sources provided by Smithsonian or even the National Holocaust Museum. For some reason, decision-makers for these public institutions chose to leave the reality of Darwinian evolution out of the resources provided to the general public.

Social and ethnic cleansing and other forms of mass extermination and violence can be laid directly at the feet of atheistic countries from the Soviet Union, where Stalin murdered an estimated twenty million people while declaring, "the new socialist man was an atheist one, free of the religious chains that had helped to bind him in class oppression."[8] *The Nanking Massacre* by Japan against China, and of course Communist

China itself, where over sixty percent of the population is atheist,[9] has committed several atrocities against its own people, especially minority ethnic and religious groups such as the Muslim Uyghurs.

Arguments by atheists that religion is the root cause of evil should concede, but rarely due, that evil is the result of the human condition and that condition is exacerbated when there is a collective opinion in society, especially among the leaders and the ruling elite, that there is no God. Unfortunately, it does not take much to motivate human beings to hurt or murder other human beings. The streets of America are inundated with gang violence where young gang members dehumanize and murder other adolescents. Women and children continue to be victims of global human sex trafficking on an unimaginable scale, and the elderly and weak are often victimized by their own families for financial gain or mere convenience. God or religion is most certainly not the cause of evil in the world.

The Human Factor

Whenever there is a discussion about ethics or morality the discussion must include the actions of one person against another person (or people). We never read about a lion being prosecuted for killing cubs so a lioness will stop lactating and be available for mating. Questions about morality or justification always involve the actions of a person, so why is this true? Darwinian evolution cannot speak to the specifics of what it means to be a human being, we really do not even know what the term "species" really means. Darwin himself wrote, "No one definition has yet satisfied all naturalists; yet every naturalist knows vaguely what he means when he speaks of species."[10] One hundred and fifty years later, scientists highlight the "continuing interest in the origin and extinction of species in that it shows what many biologists implicitly think of as real entities, even if [they] can't quite define exactly what they are."[11]

Atheism cannot clarify what makes human beings distinct. Peter Singer of Princeton University argues that self-awareness gives us the moral title of human. The problem with Singer's ontological definition of a human being is that infants i.e., two, three, four months of age, should not enjoy any more protection than an animal. Now, I dare not attribute Singer's ethic to all atheists, or for that matter, any other atheist who does not specifically express this view. However, this realization quickly stirs alarm as atheists operating from an evolutionary worldview may not be able to define a human being specifically, but they know one when they see one, regardless of age or level of development.

Divine Mandates

It has hopefully been established that evil is predominately the product of human activity with human ignorance and aggression serving as its root cause. It is necessary to now take a look at the problem of evil within the context of a theistic (Christian) worldview. The first contrast between atheism and theism is that there is a unique distinction of what it means to be a human being. The distinction of what it means to be a human being is provided in Genesis chapter one, the same chapter that references an actual beginning to our universe, although leading modern scientists did not widely accept this fact until the mid-1960s. The distinction also separates Christianity from other major religions such as Islam or Hinduism in that humanity is distinctly created in God's image.[12]

Genesis 1:26-31 describes the creation of man and woman as being both unique from the rest of creation and also being created in God's image. Genesis 1:25 records God creating the animal kingdom and he concludes that work and then he creates man and woman in his image and in His likeness. God then gives them a divine mandate to care for all of creation and to flourish in their relationship with each other. A cursory read of this chapter may cause the reader to glance over this creation event as insignificant, especially since this mandate was given in the Garden of Eden prior to the fall. However, the context of God's creation in a pre-fallen world is the standard by which to judge our fallen world.

Why is the world that we live in so hard to accept? In some respects, it is because we can fathom a world where there is no such pain and suffering. Philosophically speaking, we need good to show us what bad looks like. No one has ever observed rust just floating down a roadway, it is only been observed on the metal of a car. We look at the rust on the car and we conclude that the vehicle has not been properly maintained, stored, or cared for because we know what a nice car looks like and we have the good to compare to the bad. We know what good and bad are because we have an inherent moral compass that naturalism should not even discuss let alone thoroughly elucidate in a naturalistic worldview.

How many videos have been shown on social media of hunters rescuing a deer or other animal trapped in a fence, mud, or a frozen pond? Why would they do that? Such a weak creature obviously lacks the strength or intelligence to survive and it certainly saves the hunters' time and energy in finding something to kill and eat. What moral mechanism tells these people that it is not right to shoot an animal that is struggling to escape, but rather, something intrinsic within them compels them, even at risk to our own well-being (which is another problem of Darwinian evolution) to rescue and restore such animals to their habitat.

I would argue that in a post-fallen world, we still have a very strong affinity for God's mandate to care for creation. Most normal people, especially children, love God's creation. When I was a rescue swimmer in the Navy, we had to stage in open water in a boat just off the coast of California where we lost one of our helicopters. It was my first rescue, we had rescued three crew members, but also lost three friends and it was certainly a difficult day. As the sun began to set a large blue whale swam by the boat so close to me that I could have leaped on its back. The whale was the most magnificent sight I had ever seen. The beauty of this massive creature was transformative to me and, for some reason, a feeling of warmth and peace came over me as I watched this whale breach through the surface of the water for what seemed a long time.

Our mandate to love and care for God's creation comes easy and any violation of that inherent mandate through maltreatment or cruelty shocks the conscience and can also result in criminal confinement. Whether it is a breathtaking sunset, an animal, or our beloved pets, we absolutely love God's creation and are drawn to invest in his creation emotionally, physically, and even financially. According to multiple sources, pet owners spend well over $100 per month on their pets to care for them and treat them as part of their family. We spend significant resources to engage God's creation because we are driven to our mandate to love and care for this world, even if it is in a fallen state, our roles have been clearly defined internally.

The second mandate for Adam and Eve was to grow a family as a parent unit. Perhaps no society has trivialized the mandate for family cohesion more than Western society. We want the benefits of companionship without a serious commitment to each other and too often, the prospects of children come well after career goals and financial status. Moreover, people, such as myself, have made mistakes when having a family of being too career-oriented and not realizing how important quality time is with your spouse and children. I was fortunate as a detective to have a flexible schedule, but my time in the military, and working as a contractor to reconcile the checkbook sometimes made the role of my wife equivalent to that of a single mom.

The effects of the fall have weighed heavily on our divine mandate to care for creation and have a family, but throughout Scripture, we find that we are still considered by God to be "in his image and likeness" and so his mandates still hold true today.

If you have taken classes related to criminology, sociology, and psychology, we find the end result of failing to embrace our calling as a family unit has consequences that add to the problem of evil and suffering in our world. The U.S. Department of Justice reported in one study that "the most reliable indicator of violent crime in a community is the proportion of fatherless families."[12] The *Minnesota Psychological Association* also reports that research supports "that single-parent households experience more physical and psychological problems compared to those raised in two-parent households.[13]

Research on the negative effects of broken families is voluminous, but even with solid data supporting the institution of marriage and the family, from a non-religious vantage point, the progressive and secular worldview has systematically expressed a hostile intent toward the idea of the nuclear family. Why do so many prominent people and organizations stand in opposition to the nuclear family, which social scientists and psychologists provide data that speak to the consequences of children not having a nuclear family? Richard Weikart, European history provides an interesting insight using a name that has already been introduced, namely, Kar Marx.

Weikart ties in Marxist ideology with the abolition of the family unit. Although not anti-family, they contributed to it as a philosophical approach to family was one in which "any sexual relationship between mutually consenting persons would be possible. What would not be possible would be the security of a life-long marriage. This sexual relationship could not be chosen."[14] It does not take a philosophical leap of faith to draw the distinction between the idea that religion is the root of societal problems and the destruction of the idea that the family unit is a divine mandate not as part of a legal or moral code, but as an institution where God's image is reflected in both man and woman to its greatest extent.

The mandate by God for a man and woman to honor and

serve one another and start a family has become foreign in the minds of many Western institutions, including academia, organizations, and policymakers who strive to appease activists opposed to the idea of a man and a woman in marriage as a divine mandate. A significant portion of the problem of evil and suffering is not the result of an unloving God, but the product of an absentee father, unloving mother, and broken families in general. Many atheists or agnostics cannot begin to view God as a loving heavenly father because they have no idea what a loving father or parent is or even looks like. The psychological damage that a child or adolescent experiences as a result of the decline of the family unit is measurable.

Free-Will

The fall of Adam and Eve was the result of their willful disobedience in the Garden of Eden when they ate from the forbidden tree which God told them explicitly not to eat from. The question one might ask is, "Why did there have to be a tree?" No tree, no forbidden fruit, no temptation, no fall, and that settles the problem of evil. There is a substantial argument that sufficiently stands up against arguments for the existence or probability of an all-powerful and all-loving God in a world where evil exists. Again, it is important to stress that a philosophical theory is just that and no theory on its own, for or against God, will ever "prove" with absolute certainty, for someone holding out for that standard of proof, that God exists. Currently, the free-will defense examines the motive for God putting the possibility or potential of sin into his creation.

The philosopher Alvin Plantinga introduced the Free-Will Defense Theory in the early 1970s. His theory seeks to provide a remedy for the existence of a loving, powerful God and the phenomena of evil in the world that he created. The question is considered, could God logically create a world where there was free will and no potential for evil or possibility of rebellion by his creation? We sometimes read of philosophical questions such as, "Can God make a rock too heavy for him to lift?" Such questions are logically inconsistent and trivial to the question of God's omnipotence. Plantinga merely articulates the argument that it is not a logical inconsistency to hypothesize that God created the best possible world with free will and the potential for evil because a world with free will and evil is better than a world with no free will and no evil. The significance of this theory is not to prove the existence of God, but it is to counter the philosophical claims that many atheists embrace in that the existence of evil is "proof" for the inexistence of God.

The mystery and the depths of the logical or philosophical problem of evil have been the topic of many doctoral dissertations and books, but the intellectual gaps still remain. One could theorize that God's intellect is above ours and the fact that we cannot comprehend this mystery is of no great consequence from a philosophical vantage point, although suffering and pain or most consequential in our world. Perhaps many atheists have a problem with the presence of evil because they do not like or refuse to acknowledge God's remedy for the ontological power and existence of evil. The pain and consequences of sin and rebellion range from both moral and natural evil. In Romans 8:22, the Apostle Paul writes of the entire creation and earth groaning in pain waiting for redemption.

The issue of the problem and sin and suffering has yet another variable that too few consider. John 3:16 tells us that God freely gave his Son (Jesus Christ) to redeem us to him and deal with the consequences of sin. Jesus said in John 10:10, "No one takes my life, I give my life of my own free will." When Jesus was praying in the Garden of Gethsemane right before the dawn of his crucifixion, he cried out, "If possible, let this cup pass from my hand, but not my will, but yours will be done." God's justice for sin was being heaped on the head of Jesus to remove the curse of sin in the first part of our redemption, spiritual life for all eternity, and then he was raised from the tomb and resurrected as the "first-fruits" of our resurrection in a new heaven and a new earth where we read, "Now the dwelling of God is with man." *Revelation 21:3.*

If we want to ponder the problem of evil then we should ultimately ask, "Why is our Creator on a cross?" Why is the one who spoke our universe and life into existence, the divine *Logos* (John 1:1), being beaten, spit upon, mocked, tortured, and executed for crimes or sins he never committed. And why do men still hate him today? You can talk about "God," but the name of Jesus often evokes the same hatred and spite today, especially among our educated elite, as it did when he was nailed to the cross.

Examining the Evidence:

We know from the Bible that God created man and woman in his image in a perfect environment. The environment was perfect because there was free will in paradise. We also know that the result of the fall was God's provisional plan of sending Jesus into the world to redeem humanity unto himself. In this pattern, which is similar to Israel's pattern throughout Scripture, we find ourselves in a covenant with God, rebellion, calamity, and suffering turning us back to God, and deliverance and restoration by God's hand alone.

The evil and suffering we experience in this life are profound. The hurt, pain, and loss leave indelible marks upon our lives that some will carry until the setting of this present life. However, we should consider the options. First, God, knowing all things, including the future, could have simply not created humanity. However, at great cost, he still breathed air into Adam's lungs and then walked Adam's wife, Eve, to be by his side to start the human race. Second, God could have just wiped Adam and Eve out and started again. When he told them that they would die from their sin, instead of starting a plan of redemption, he could have taken Adam and Eve's life immediately. However, God gave them coverings, he gave them a family, and Adam and Eve retained the image of God in their lives. Ultimately, this pathway would lead to the cross and the death of Christ.

"Therefore, just as through one man sin entered into the world, and death through sin, and so death spread to all mankind, because all sinned— for until the Law sin was in the world, but sin is not counted against anyone when there is no law. Nevertheless, death reigned from Adam until Moses, even over those who had not sinned in the likeness of the violation committed by Adam, who is a type of Him who was to come."

Romans 5:12-14

Notes

Chapter 1: Deliberate Skepticism

1 James Moreland, Williams L. Craig, *Philosophical Foundations for a Christian Worldview* (Intervarsity Press, 2003), 94.
2 www.atheistscholar.org/AtheistPhilosophies/LogicalPositivism.aspx
3 Phil Hilts, "Lifting the Curtain on the Cosmic Egg and the Big Bang" *The Washington Post*. February 16, 1978.
4 Richard Dawkins, *The Blind Watchmaker* (W. W. Norton & Company, 2015), 1.
5 www.dailymotion.com/video/x5ruzde
6 Richard Lewinton, *Billions and Billions of Demons*, The New York Review, January 9, 1997.
7 David Berlinski, *The Devil's Delusion: Atheism and its Scientific Pretensions* (Crown Forum, 2008).
8 https://www.bethinking.org/does-science-disprove-god/turning-science-faith-debate-on-its-head.
9 John Gray, *Straw Dogs: Thoughts on Humans and Other Animals*, (Granta Books, 2007), 26.
10 John Horgan, *Can Faith and Science Coexist? Mathematician and Christian John Lennox Responds*, Scientific American, March 1, 2015.
11 https://conversantfaith.com/2014/04/28/20-quotes-from-mind-and-cosmos-by-thomas-nagel/
12 Linda Murawski, *Critical Thinking in the Classroom... and Beyond*, Journal of Learning in Higher Education 10(1), 2014.
13 The Stanford Encyclopedia of Philosophy "Critical Thinking" recovered from https://plato.stanford.edu/entries/critical-thinking/.
14 Ana-Maria Šimundić, *Bias in Research*, Biochemia Medica, 23(1), 2013, 12.
15 Raymond Nickerson, Confirmation Bias: A Ubiquitous Phenomenon in Many Guises, Review of General Psychology, 2(2), 1998,175.

16 Baijayanta Roy, *Confirmation Bias in the sciences – A Double-Edged Sword*, Srikanth Sugavanam, April 20, 2017.

17 Richard Harris, *Rigor Mortis: How Sloppy Science Creates Worthless Cures, Crushes Hopes, and Wastes Billions*, (Basic Books, 2017).

18 Harry Crane, Ryan Martin, *Academia's Case of Stockholm Syndrome*, Quillette, 29 November 2018. www.quillette.com/2018/11/29/academias-case-of-stockhold-syndrome/.

19 https://retractionwatch.com.

Chapter 2: Defining Your Worldview

1 B.B. Wolman, *Dictionary of Behavioral Science*, (New York, 1973), in Mark Koltko-Rivera, *The Psychology of Worldviews*, Review of General Psychology, 8(1), 2004.

2 W. F., Overton, W. F., Historical and contemporary perspectives on developmental theory and research strategies. 1991, In R. M. Downs, L. S. Liben, & D. S. Palermo (Eds.), Visions of aesthetics, the environment and development (pp. 263–311). Hillsdale, NJ: Erlbaum

3 Norman L. Geisler, *The Big Book of Christian Apologetics: An A-to-Z Guide*, (Baker Books, 2012).

4 www.socratic.org/questions/what-is-the-cost-of-a-human-body-in-terms-of-the-different-elements-that-make-it.

5 www.marktwainstudies.com

6 Richard Dawkins, "Richard Dawkins on Terrorism & Religion" NPR, *Weekend Edition*.

7 Andrew Anthony, *Sam Harris, the new atheist with a spiritual side*, The Guardian.

8 Lawrence Rifkin, *Is the meaning of your life to make babies?* Scientific America.

9 Richard Dawkins, *River Out of Eden: A Darwinian View of Life*, (Basic Books, 1996).

10 Kerby Anderson, *Atheists and Their Fathers*, https://probe.org/atheists-and-their-fathers/, May 27, 2002.

11 https://www.theway.co.uk/news/atheism-a-delusion-say-prof--john-lennox.

12 Jeff Long. *Near-Death Experiences: Evidence for their reality.* Missouri Medicine, 111(5), 2014, 378.

13 Kendra Cherry, *The Asch Conformity Experiments*, www.verywellmind. com, April 3, 2020.

14 www.reddit.com

15 St John's College, University of Cambridge. "One of Darwin's evolution theories finally proved." ScienceDaily. www.sciencedaily. com/releases/2020/03/200317215626.htm

16 Richard Dawkins, *The God Delusion*, (Transworld Publishing, 2006).

17 Cara Buckley, *Man is rescued by Stranger on Subway Tracks*, New York Times, January 3, 2007.

18 Josh Cole, *True Happiness is Found in Helping Others*, June 9, 2016, https://www.medium.com/@SaikoJosh/true-happiness-is-found-in-helping-others-3c1314353d4f

Chapter 3: Revolution for Evolution

1   T. Ryan Gregory. *Understanding Natural Selection: Essential Concepts and Common Misconceptions*. Evo Edu Outreach 2, 2009,156.

2   Ernst Mayr, *Darwin's Influence on Modern Thought*, Scientific American, November 29, 2009.

3   Ibid

4   Evolution Topic: Intellectually fulfilled atheists? (counterbalance.org)

5   https://ncse.ngo

6   Richard Weikert, *From Darwin to Hitler*, (Palgrave MacMillan, 2006).

7   Matti Leisola & Jonathan Witt, *Heretic: One Scientist's Journey from Darwin to Design*, (Discovery Institute, 2018), 46.

8   Sam Harris. "The Moral Landscape: How Science can Determine Human Values. New York, NY (Free Press), 2010, 11.

9   Ian Hesketh and Henry-James Meiring, *Guide to the classics: Darwin's The Descent of Man 150 years on — sex, race and our 'lowly' ape ancestry*. The Conversation, 2021.

10 *Ibid.*

11 Steven A. Gelb. *Darwin's Use of Intellectual Disability in the Descent of Man, Disability Studies*, 2008, 28(2).

12 *Ibid.*

13 Charles Darwin, *The Descent of Man, And Selection in Relation to Sex*, 1871.

14 Wudan Yan, *Charles Darwin was one sick dude*, JSTOR Daily, 2016.

15 Campbell AK, Matthews SB Darwin's illness revealed *Postgraduate Medical Journal* 2005;81:248-251.

16 https://www.nature.com/scitable/forums/genetics-generation/america-s-hidden-history-the-eugenics-movement-123919444/.

17 www.in.gov IHB: 1907 Indiana Eugenics Law

18 https://criminologyweb.com/cesare-lombroso-theory-of-crime-criminal-man-and-atavism/.

19 John Conley, *Margaret Sanger's Extreme Brand of Eugenics*, America: The Jesuit Review, July 28, 2020.

20 Nikita Stewart, *Planned Parenthood in N.Y. Disavows Margaret Sanger Over Eugenics, The New York Times, July 21, 2020.*

21 *Aktion T4 the Nazi euthanasia programme that killed 300,000*, www.history.co.uk.

22 Richard Weikart, *From Darwin to Hitler: Evolutionary Ethics, Eugenics and racism in Germany*, (Palgrave Macmillan, 4th ed., 2006).

23 Robert J. Lifton, *The Nazi Doctors*, (Basic Books, 1986), 4.

24 Viktor E. Frankl, "The Doctor and the Soul: From Psychotherapy to Logotherapy," (Richard Winston and Clara Winston: Translator), Vintage, 1986.

25 Ben Prawdzik, *Milgram Experiment, 50 years on,* Yale News, September 28, 2011.

26 Omar Haque, Julian De Feitas, Ivana Viani, Bradly Niederschulte, Harold Bursztajn, *Why Did So Many German Doctors Joint the Nazi Party Early?* International Journal of Law and Psychiatry, 35, 473.

27 Tara Kibler, The Complicated History of Eugenics in the United States, HeinOnline blog, June 11, 2021. https://home.heinonline.org/blog/2021/06/the-complicated-history-of-eugenics-in-the-united-states/.

28 Jordan Boyd, Justice Sonia Sotomayor Gruesomely Compares Unborn Babies to Being Brain Dead, The Federalist, December 1,2021.

29 Peter Gluckman, Felicia Low, Tatjana Buklijas, Mark Hanson, Alan Beedle, *How evolutionary principles improve the understanding of human health and disease, Evol Appl.* 4(2), 2011, 249-263.

Chapter 4: Evolution: Flaws & Faith

1   Sherwin, F. 2009. "No Weaknesses in the Theory of Evolution?" *Institute of Creation Research.*

2   Richard Dawkins, *Prospect*, March 11, 2013.

3   Haeckel E. Last words on evolution. New York: Peter Eckler; 1906. Recovered from Pereto, J & Catala, J. 2012. "Darwinism and the Origin of Life" *Evolution: Education and Outreach 5*, 337-341.

4   P.V. Sukumaran, *Cambrian Explosion of Life: The Big Bang in Metazoan Evolution*, Resonance, 2004, 38.

5   Richard Dawkins. *The Blind Watchmaker*, (Norton & Company, 1986), 284.

6   Ibid.

7   J.W. Valentine. *The prelude to the Cambrian explosion*. Annual Review of Earth and Planetary Sciences, 30, 285.

8   George Klein. 1990. The Atheist in the Holy City: Encounters and Reflections, 203.

9   Frederick J. Heeren, *Was the final craniate on the road to recognition?* Evolution and Cognition 9(2), 2003, 142.

10   *Ibid*

11   Phillip E. Johnson, *The Church of Darwin*, The Wall Street Journal, August 16, 1992.

12   Shea, John. 2011. "Refuting a myth about human origins." American Scientific 99/2, p.128.

13   Amos Wollen, *Darwin's "horrid" doubt, in context, History and Philosophy of the Life Sciences, 42 (102). This article was used to quote Darwin's "horrid doubt," but was used to argue against standard interpretations on Darwin's commentary. However, this article was republished after multiple corrections related to specific historical quotes* and their content.

14   https://evolutionnews.org/2015/03/why_evolutionar/.

15   Rolls, Edmund. On the Relations between the Mind and the Brain: A Neuroscience Perspective. *Philosophia Scientiæ, 17 (2)*, 2013, 32.

16   *Ibid*, 31-70.

17   Richard Klein, *The Atheist and the Holy City: Encounters and Reflections*, (MIT Press, 1992). 203.

18   *Scientists and Belief*, 2009. Recovered from Scientists and Belief. *Pew Research Center* (pewforum.org).

Chapter 5: Scientism

1   Thomas Burnett, *What is Scientism?* Dialogue on Science and Religion, May 21, 2012.

2   Ibid.

3   Peter Medawar, *Advice to a Young Scientist*, (Harper Row, 1979), 31

4   Matthew Reisz, *Is Philosophy Dead?* February 22, 2015.

5   Renai Gasparatou, *Scientism and Scientific Thinking*, Science and Education, 26(3),1

6   Isaac Newton, *Principia Mathematica*.

7   https://www.goodreads.com/author/quotes/79396.johannes_kepler.

8   J.J. MacIntosh, and Peter Anstey, "Robert Boyle", *The Stanford Encyclopedia of Philosophy* (Winter 2018 Edition).

9   John Lennox, When things just don't fit: Science and the Easter faith, April 13, 2012.

10   *Miracles* by CS Lewis © copyright CS Lewis Pte Ltd 1947, 1960. Extract used with permission.

11   Albert Einstein. "Physics and Reality," *Journal of the Franklin Institute* 221, no. 3 (March 1936), 349–382. Reprinted in *Ideas and Opinions*, 292. Used with Permission.

12   Stephen Hawking, *Brief Answers to Big Questions*, (John Murry, 2018).

13   Steve Conner, *Martin Rees: "We shouldn't attach any weight to what Hawking says about god," www.independent.co.uk.*

14   Richard Feynman, The Value of Science, Engineering and Science, 1955.

15   Kimberly Winston, Carl Sagan, The Cosmos Will Be, Religion News, March 5, 2014.

16   www.johnlennox.org, January 23, 2019.

17   Michael Holden, God did not create the universe, says Hawking, Reuters, September 2, 2020.

18   John Lennox vs Peter Atkins debate: Can science explain everything? - YouTube

19   William G. Mitchener, *The Nature of Mathematics*, https://services.math.duke.edu.

20   Andrew Zhuravchak, *Do We Need Math? Imagine Life Without It*, www.medium.com, January 18, 2020.

Chapter 6: Modus Operandi

1   Richard Dawkins, The God Delusion, Mariner Books, 2008.

2   Ibid.

3   Christopher Hitchens, *https://imgur.com/gallery/SXGE100.*

4   Frank Turek vs David Silverman – The Reality Debate Christian Debate Analysis.

5   Geoffrey Marcaggi and Fabian Guenole, Freudarwin: Evolutionary Thinking as a Root Cause of Psychoanalysis, Front Psychol, 2018, 2.

6   Ibid.

7   Stephen J. Padilla, A Psychology of Atheism: can Merit be Found in the "Defective Father Hypothesis."

8   Anthony Hitchens, god is not great,

9   Kerby Anderson, Atheists and Their Father. Probe for Answers, 2020.

10 Ralph Blumenthal, Freud: Secret Documents Reveal Years of Strife, The New York Times, January 24, 1984.

11 Stephen J. Padilla, A Psychology of Atheism: can Merit be Found in the "Defective Father Hypothesis."

12 Richard Dawkins, Childhood, Abuse, and the Escape from Religion: The Case of Edgardo Mortara, 2018.

13 In his book "the God Delusion," Dawkins only sites one source dealing with psychology. You would think that the word "delusion," being in the title of the book would be defined instead of relying on popular culture to define the term. Furthermore, he fails to even put the term in context in his book or his index.

14 Richard Dawkins, The God Delusion, (Boston, Houghton Mifflin, 2006) 347.

15 https://kidadl.com/articles/christopher-hitchens-quotes-from-the-british-critic-and-writer

16 Rob Whitley, *Religion and Mental Health: What is the Link?* Psychology Today, December 18, 2017.

17 Paul Mueller, David Plevak, and Teresa Rummans, *Religious Involvement, Spirituality, and Medicine: Implications for Clinical Practice*, Mayo Clin Proc, 76, 2001, 1225.

18 Ibid, 1229.

19 Kate Mossman, *Richard Dawkins interview: "What I say in biology has become pretty much orthodoxy,"* The New Statesman, UK ed., December 9, 2021.

Chapter 7: Not a Chance?

1   Louis Mead and Eugenie Scott, Problem Concepts in Evolution Part II: Cause and Chance, Evo Edu Outreach, 201, 3, 263.

2   Ibid

3   Christie Wilcox, Evolution: A Game of Chance, Scientific American, January 11, 2012.

4   Abiogenesis Theory Explained - HRF (healthresearchfunding.org).

5   Abiogenesis (allaboutscience.org).

6   Stephen D. Meyer, Signature in the Cell, (Harper Collins Publishing, 2009), 219.

7   *Ibid.*

8   Joji M. Otaki, Shunsuke Ienaka, Tomonori Gotoh, Haruhiko Yamamato, Availability of short amino acid sequences in proteins, Protein Science 14(3), 618.

9   Douglas Fox, *Primordial Soup's On: Scientists Repeat Evolution's Most Famous Experiment*, Scientific American, March 28, 2007.

10 Ibid.

11 https://www.khanacademy.org/science/ap-biology/natural-selection/origins-of-life-on-earth/a/hypotheses-about-the-origins-of-life.

12 Helen Fields, *The Origins of Life*, Smithsonian Magazine, October 2010 https://www.smithsonianmag.com/science-nature/the-origins-of-life-60437133/.

13 Stephen Meyer, Signature in the Cell, (Harper Collins Publishing, 2009), 244.

14 *Ibid.*

15 Matti Leisola and Jonathan Witt, Heretic: One Scientist's Journey from Darwin to Design, (Discovery Press Institute, 2018), 39.

16 https://www.goodreads.com/quotes/336336-dna-is-like-a-computer-program-but-far-far-more.

17 Michael Behe, *Reply to my critics: A response to reviews of Darwin's Black Box: the biochemical challenge to evolution*, Biology and Philosophy, 16.

18 Evolutionnews.org/2013/06/did_scientists_/.

19 Michael Behe, Irreducible Complexity: Obstacle to Darwinian Evolution, https://www.lehigh.edu/~inbios/Faculty/Behe/PDF/Behe_chapter.pdf.

20 Charles Darwin, *On the Origin of Species*, 213.

21 Michael Behe, Reply to my critics: A response to reviews of Darwin's Black Box: the biochemical challenge to evolution, Biology and Philosophy, 16.

22 Darwin's Eye Quote, https://www.scienceagainstevolution.org/v14i9e.htm.

23   S. Kojima and D.F. Blair, *The bacterial flaPretentiousgellar motor: structure and function of a complex molecular machine.* Int Rev Cytol. 2004.

24   Franklin M. Harold, The Way of the Cell: Molecules, Organisms and the Order of Life, (Oxford University Press, 2001), 2015.

25   Tim Folger, Science's Alternative to an Intelligent Creator: The Multiverse Theory, Discover Magazine, November 10, 2008.

26   Ella Anderson, Multiverse: The Anthropic Principle, December 4, 2019, https://medium.com/predict/multiverse-the-anthropic-principle-fab3a09409ad.

27   Ibid.

28   Mariette Le Roux and Laurence Coustal, After Death, Hawking cuts "multiverse" theory down to size, https://phys.org/news/2018-05-death-hwaking-multiverse-theory-size.html, May 6, 2018.

29   John Lennox, God's Undertaker: Has Science Burred God? (Lion Hudson, 2009), 156.

30   God's Undertaker is one of the most prolific and easy reads of Dr. Lennox's work covering a vast array of topics related to Christian apologetics.

31   https://www.youtube.com/watch?v=QmIc42oRjm8.

Chapter 8: Has God Really Said?

1   Scot McKnight, War Language as Hyperbole: "Total-Kill," Christianity Today, March 10, 2020.

2   E.W. Bullinger, Figures of Speech Used in the Bible (Grand Rapids, Baker Books, 1968), https://crossexamined.org/godbuster-debate-elliot-george/.

3   Jimena, Ezer Kenegdo, February 22, 2018. https://ezerkenegdo.org/ezer-kenegdo/

4   Lawrence Mykytiuk, *Archaeology Confirms 50 Real People in the Bible,* Biblical Archaeology Review, 40:2, March/April 2014.

5   Sidnie White Crawford, *"Has Every Book of the Bible Been Found Among the Dead Sea Scrolls?"* Bible Review 12:5, October 1996.

6   https://logos.com/how-to/study-nt-mss.

7   *Hasn't archaeology disproved the Bible?* Infostudenti.net

8   Davies, P. R.. "Dead Sea Scrolls." *Encyclopedia Britannica,* July 26, 2021. https://www.britannica.com/topic/Dead-Sea-Scrolls.

Chapter 9: Miracles

1   David Hume. *An Inquiry Concerning Human Understanding*, 1748. Note, Hume was not an atheist, but in fact, in *Dialogues Concerning Natural Religion*, Hume's argument through the character *Philo*, according to Jerry Walls, insisted that God's existence is virtually self-existent, but only the moral agency of God was in doubt. Jerry W. Walls, "Hume on Divine Amorality," *Religious Studies*, 26, 257.

2   Descartes, *Meditation One (1641)*, https://www.wmpeople.wm.edu/asset/index/cvance/ descartes.

3   Joan E. Taylor. Jesus as News: Crises of Health and Overpopulation in Galilee. *Journal for the Study of New Testament 44(1)*, 2021.

4   IVP New Testament Commentary Series, John.

5   Francis Watson 'Historical Evidence' and the Resurrection of Jesus. *Theology*. 1987, p.365.

6   Michael J. O. Andrade. Do congenitally blind people have visual dreams? *Sleep Science*, 2021, p.191.

7   Kenneth Ring and Sharron Cooper. Near-Death and Out-of-Body-Experiences in the Blind: A study of apparent eyeless vision. *The Journal of Near-Death Studies*, 1997.

Chapter 10: Evil and Suffering

1   Richard Dawkins. *The God Delusion*, Mariner Books, 2008.

2   Ibid, 309.

3   Rutledge M. Dennis. *Social Darwinism, Scientific Racism, and the Metaphysics of Race, The Journal of Negro Education*, 64(3), 1995. Pp 243-252.

4   Natasha Frost, Why Stalin Tried to Stamp Out Religion in the Soviet Union. Recovered from www.history.com.

5   Darwin, Africa, and Genocide: The Horror of Scientific Racism, *YouTube*.

6   Charles Darwin, *The Descent of Man,* 1871.

7   William Dembski, Casey Luskin, Joseph Holden, *The Comprehensive Guide to Science and Faith,* (Harvest House), 391.

8   Chief Editor, Why Stalin Tried to Stamp Out Religion in the Soviet Union, https:// www.dailyhindnews.com. April 23, 2021.

9   Kimberly Winston, *The Once Officially Atheist China is booming with Religion*. America: Justice Review, May 18, 2017.

10 Charles Darwin, On The Origin of Species, 1859

11 Sadeer el-Showk, Do Species Really Exist? Accumulating Glitches: Exploring the Grandeur of Evolution. https://www.nature.com/scitable/blog/accumulating-glitches/

12 The Imago Dei or "Image of God" in mankind speaks to the functional and relational aspects of mankind with God while serving as vice-regent over God's creation. Further study in Anthony Hoekema's *Created in God's Image* is recommended for anyone desiring a greater understanding of this theological concept.

13 R. L. Maginnis, Single-Parent Families Cause Juvenile Crime. U.S. DOJ, Office of Justice Programs

14 Jerod Brown, *Father-Absent Homes: Implications for Criminal Justice and Mental Health Professionals*. Minnesota Psychological Association.

15 Richard Weikart, Marx, Engels, and the Abolition of Family, History of European Ideas, 18(5), 1994,

Made in the USA
Columbia, SC
30 July 2023

21045164R00098